INDIA VISION

NEW AGE EQUALITY

INDIA VISION

NEW AGE EQUALITY

Kapil Gupta
Bhushan Bhati

Prints Publications Pvt Ltd
New Delhi

Published by

Prints Publications Pvt Ltd
Viraj Tower-2, 4259/3, Ansari Road,
Darya Ganj, New Delhi-110002
Tel. : +91-11-45355555
Fax: +91-11-23275542
E-mail : contact@printspublications.com
Website : www.printspublications.com

First Edition : 2021 (Paperback)

ISBN 978-81-927694-4-8

Price : ₹ 195/-

Published and Printed by Mr. Pranav Gupta (Director) on behalf of Prints Publications Pvt Ltd at Mohit Enterprises, Delhi.

Contents

PREFACE

I have grown up reading about power and what it means and what it does to people. Power was taught sometimes as money and sometimes as derived from control. However, the more I have delved into India, the more I realize how untrue this is.

India is a country run by the mob or the fear of the mob. It's not a country run by the politicians, it's not a country run by the businessmen. All the businessmen try to do is control the politicians and all politicians want to do is to have a mechanism to control the mob.

A logical question is: What is the mob? The mob is not a group of people, it's a cause or initiative. Being a politician essentially means having a mechanism to continuously keep coming up with a cause or initiative.

It's so much so, that even liberals in this country are part of a mob. Sometimes, the more dangerous mob!

The liberals, who by definition should be part of non-alignment, who should always be open to consider, open to debate, open to listen, are part of a mob hell-bent on having their way. For Neanderthals like me, this goes against the very definition of liberal but then I am too much of a centrist (according to their definition) to talk over liberals. Anyway, that's a debate for some other book.

I have had a unique vantage point over the last few years to work closely with the Indian polity but never become part of it. Coupled with my global experiences, I am using this book as an attempt to list out some aspects needed to push India into the right development cycle. While saying this, I realize that India may mean different for different people. Is it the land or the people; if it's the people, then which people? Who defines and completes India?

As you read through this book, some of this will get answered and what doesn't get answered will remain as an enquiry for the readers to define for themselves. And that's the beauty of it. You get to define it for yourself.

Kapil Gupta

Introduction by the Co-Author

India Vision was an accident, something that I never intended to write but ended up writing quite a bit. This book, while it might not be an actual representation of my thoughts, is something that I have started to believe in.

When I began working on the book, it almost felt like I was reading something so profound that it would either provoke the reader or imbue them with a perspective that they won't be able to challenge. The idea of a perfect India was something that I had always wanted to curate but with my limited knowledge and ability to propagate, I never went ahead with it, until now.

You can call me a GEN-Y or GEN-Z human, I was born in the 90s and till the early years of the past decade, I had little to no interest in politics. It was some 7-8 years ago that I developed an active interest in the workings of the government and how their conduct directly affects my daily life.

I am not an activist but I am not a dud either. If something needs to be said, I will say it but not at the cost of my own mental well being. I guess, this book breaks that rule. The only single thought that I had in my mind whilst working on this book was how many people am I going to offend? Going by the current state of affairs in the country, it was hard not to think about if people would chase me after getting their sentiments hurt but I continued to work on it anyway. Not because I am not scared, but because for once, I would like to convey my opinion without fear.

Around a year or so ago, I stopped putting my voice out on social media because I was convinced that it's not safe anymore to do so, but this book changes all that.

The thing that you need to keep in mind while reading this is that India Vision may not be your vision or my vision, to be honest, I partly disagree with it, but, it is the vision that is required for this country to catapult itself to the next level. We need to understand that we as a country, like to live in denial and it is time that we face our demons head on, with all our glory.

As you foray into the book, you will find things that you will disagree with, things that may make your blood boil, but that is the point of this. Somebody had to come in and tell you all these things, because acceptance is virtue and we need to accept and act.

If it makes your blood boil, it is indeed the truth.

Bhushan Bhati

ACKNOWLEDGEMENT

This book has been a long time coming. It didn't really start as India Vision. It started as a tell tale of my experiences with people in power, while I was doing political social media campaigning for national and state elections in India.

And then somewhere the mission changed and it got rewritten. Thanks to the set of wonderful people around me. The team at OMLogic. People have come and gone within this team but their contribution can not be stated enough. Special mention must go to Bhushan Bhati for saving this book from become an unfinished and forever WIP. He truly pulled me through to completion while making a significant contribution as a co-author of the book.

Key mentions must be made of contributions from Ira, Nidhi, Navita, Vaishnavi, Ruchi and others. They all ensured they help without making me change the viewpoint. A special thank you to Prints Publications and my dear friend Pranav Gupta for publishing this.

Thank you must be done to all those who have given me all the good, bad, ugly experiences over the last few years that have given me the power, the wisdom and the vision to write this. Finally, thanks to all the readers. Please connect with me @kapgup to keep the conversation going.

Chapter 1

Equality and Entitlement

The theme of life per me is EQUALITY. Ensuring everyone is treated equally, people with abilities and/or disabilities, people with all differentiated qualities, behaviours, or the generally accepted gender/sex/race/religion/caste/orientation/pronouns.

The reason this chapter is chapter 0 is because the train of my thoughts begins from the station named Equality and anything and everything flows through there and what doesn't definitely has to make a stop. What does being treated equally mean, is where I stop being a 'Liberal'.

The fundamental issue with India starts with its political and social structure. We live in the world of entitlement. It started right when India gained its freedom, and we were taught to stand up. Wrongfully though, we have never been taught to stand down.

From Bollywood to our education to everything we have ever been told, we are entitled to everything. And someone has to figure out how to give it to us. From a movie like 'Naya Daur' to whatever story we have ever been told, Indian socialism has gone from bad to worse.

Socialism in the 20th century was the order of the day. It was needed. It was the time of oppression. It was the time where ensuring equal opportunities, reservations, ensuring the development of poor people was both needed for their development as well as for the development of the society. It was something they deserved, something that was provided to them.

However, in the 21st century, it has become an entitlement. It's not just the poor, it's not just the underprivileged. This entitlement is part of all of us. We expect to be served on the platter, with no responsibilities. We have entitlements as farmers, as government employees, as army-men, as unions, as any community or aggregation of a group of people.

This is what I referred to as the mob. This is what distinguishes us from the rest of the world. I want you all to read this and think about all the times you used some entitlement in your life.

I once talked to a former Indian minister for minorities and he quoted an interesting instance of the *Jain* community coming to ask for reservations as a minority. His basic issue with this request was not whether Jains of the country were a minority or not, his issue was that he didn't know any (A SINGLE) poor, economically backward or socially oppressed Jain.

For me this is not an instance of reservation, this is an instance of the rule of the mob.

We have somehow perceived equality as ability for everyone to get equal everything. That's not equality, at least not the way humans were built. We are supposed to be competitive, we are supposed to earn everything. Creating an environment of equality is good, overdoing it creates a reason for people to not work hard. For people to not give their best. And that's inhumane. As inhumane as anything could be. Equality should not become a medium to put down the high flyers, the top achievers.

Equality is not creating an environment where everyone gets everything. Equality is not food security, equality is not farm waivers, equality is not subsidies, equality is not free this and free that. Simply put, equality is equal opportunity. Equality is the measure of number of lifetimes it takes for a person of ability to make it from bottom to the top. It is not the availability of food, water, clothes and shelter to everyone. Socialism at its core creates more inequality in the society than anything else.

(pure socialism is not possible and is not the baseline of this comment.)

We are still living in a 20th Century version of equality, it's time to renew our equality pledge to 21st Century dynamics.

Chapter 2

The Diverse India

Since time immemorial we have read the phrase 'unity in diversity' when we talk about India. So much so that it has become a slogan. The diversity factor/criteria, in general, differs from country to country and time to time. Talking about India, in particular, its cultural and political context makes it different from any other place in the world.

To quote Tharoor in this backdrop, "in India we celebrate the commonality of major differences. If America is a melting-pot, then to me India is a thali, a selection of sumptuous dishes in different bowls. Each tastes different, and does not necessarily mix with the next, but they belong together on the same plate, and they complement each other in making the meal a satisfying repast."

So how do policies and rules function in a geography which is so huge and stands as starkly as Himalayas stand to Kanya Kumari? We could go into the deep plunges of discussion around religion, caste and ethnicity and so on and so forth, but let's not go there. Many have said and traversed across that crossroad.

Lets instead talk about the demarcations of urban, rural and semi-urban. The three differ from each other on several pointers- population, literacy rate, cultural backbone, sex ratio, employment difference, quality of living, pace of life, satisfaction rate and so on. However, RBI made this classification easy for themselves when they defined the guidelines for branch allocation.

Based on the size of the population, a centre, where bank branch is located, is classified either into rural, semi-urban, urban, or metropolitan as under:

Rural: population less than 10,000

Semi-Urban: 10,000 and above and less than 1 lakh

Urban: 1 lakh and above and less than 10 lakh

Metropolitan: 10 lakh and above

Simple and convenient, isn't it? But when we talk about reforms and policies for a better India, such demarcations and its various governing factors just cannot be ignored (If the policies are curated with the aim of actually making a difference and bringing a positive change).

What are policies and reforms made for? To address problem statements and provide a solution. Right? When the problem statements keep changing from one marked territory to another, how possibly can the solution be one. So, let's address the elephant in the room and talk about every factor that we feel important at this point of time. (Given that timeline is subjected to change- it could be possible that after some time, some of the factors listed might go redundant or some new factors may crop up).

The Division

Let's just make it clear before we dive into the depth of demographic studies that division of land/ settlements/ areas and so on is more of a political phenomenon than being based on economic factors.

Region	Definition	RC & M Specific
Urban (100+ cities)	All statutory places with a Municipalities, corporation, cantonment board or notified town area committee, etc.	All locatiobns with a population of 5 lac+ i.e. Metros, State Capitals, Top 5 cities of every state.
Semi Urban (300+ Towns)	Sorrounding residential areas of a bigger city, a group of these can collectively be regarded as the suburbs, generally they pertain to residential districts	All Locations with a population of 1 lac - 5 lac i.e. District Headquarters, Tehsils
Rural (4000+ Blocks)	Areas with Population density < 400 sq. km., or where 75% of the male working population is engaged in agriculture, or areas with no Municipal corporation/Board	All locations with a population of less than 1 lac i.e. Blocks, Villages

First ever so-called definition of Indian urban was sketched based on high population density in 1961. However, it was soon realised that a census based on population parameters will soon transcend the boundaries.

Let us, now, establish the ground for our divisions.

a) Urban, Semi-urban and rural as three divisions aren't static, but fluid. There is a constant influx of people migrating, both permanent and temporary.

b) Most of the settlements have a strong societal backbone with huge emphasis on religious and social norms. This stays the most relevant to rural, semi-urban and to some or no extent to urban (in the same order).

c) The need for employment remains to be the driving force for movement of people or migration from one division to another.

d) Educational opportunities are another parameter that attracts youth from semi-urban areas to urban areas for personal and professional growth.

Urban

Under the canopy of urbanization and peri-urbanization, the urban houses almost 370 million people of the country. The ever sprawling, densely populated urban settlement with its offsprings mushrooming at the periphery of the city is always trying to mesh with its borders. Rampant migration of people from semi-urban to urban space for career and lifestyle opportunities not only adds to the number of feet running on the metro pavements, it also adds the status classification in the all so class-conscious group of people. However, discrimination based on caste, creed or religion is not an issue in the fast-paced urban world. Hence, the idea of reservations in this space almost seems mindless. Spatial development can always be seen in the form of infrastructure as there is always a void to fill for the elite amusement- a new club, or a high-end society.

While urban is supposed and assumed to be on the top of the pyramid- it comes with its own woes and problems. Overcrowding has led to creation of slums and poor living conditions for people. If we were to give you a number, 17.4 percent of all urban households live in slums. They live in squashed suburbs, lack of basic amenities like proper sanitation and clean drinking water is just the beginning of their problems. Owning a flat in metropolitans is extremely difficult except when you own a slum (jhuggi).

Semi Urban

Most of the Indian population occupies a middle ground away from the city scrapers and village buckets. These are what we term as semi-urban. These areas can too require the services of an urban settlement, given the large settlements. But, because of many politico-economic factors that are denied by the government, they remain unbenefited.

The semi-urban male is a person who starts earning at a young age to become family man. Television ads and hoardings used to be his primary source of information however Social Media is bridging a lot of gaps. The possible occupations are bank clerk, shop owner, school teacher, accountant or a factory worker. The annual income is considerably less when compared with their urban counterpart. Exposure through media is creating a desire to improve lifestyle. Respect from family and society is the most important factor for the semi-urban male.

A semi-urban female is eventually opening doors for herself and exercising the agency of choice in 'selected areas and categories.' She is literate mostly being graduates and is shifting towards a paradigm of being more career oriented- teacher, nurse, small scale food business etc. being her options. The women are happy and content with their lifestyle. They are comfortable in going out in groups and seek similar company.

While the semi-urban seem like blissful utopia, there are a number of pain points. The one on the top is discrimination on the basis of class. While the problem is not as harsh as seen in the rural settlements, the element subconsciously is ingrained in the minds of the people. How many times have you heard people say, 'it is because of (names a community) that we are facing this problem. When we (refers of his community) were in majority some years ago, things were a lot better' or '(names a particular community) have ruined the name of our city'? Yes, that is exactly what we are trying to put in the context.

Rural

Given the increasing rate of urbanization in last 2 decades, the percentage population living in rural areas went down from 76% to 70%. Yet, two third of the of India's total population still lives in rural areas. Poor electricity, lack of quality education, and non-existent healthcare is just the beginning of the problems for rural India. Open defecation and lack of basic sanitation facilities not only leads to unhealthy conditions, it also becomes a source of various diseases and contaminations.

Your caste, your gender, your relations with the village money lender, your economic state- all are MAJOR factors that decide how you live in the settlement. Agriculture, as we all know, is more or less the main source of income for the people. Hence their life, in a way, revolves around how the crop performs, the weather conditions, and so on. The other non-farm employment options are labour oriented, or small scaled businesses.

Discrimination on the basis of caste, creed and religion still lurks like a ghost in the dain pathways of the area. Honour killings, caste-based oppressions and crimes hardly make it to the pages of the newspaper you read. The historically marginalized and oppressed scheduled casts and scheduled tribes and the crimes conflicted on them by the upper-class remains to be prevalent.

What does it mean for India's development?

The non-inclusion of this diversity inclusion in major Indian policies essentially renders a lot ineffective. India is not ONE. Any initiative, from a policy to a taxation to a development, need to be defined keeping in mind whom it is being defined for. Rural India may suffer from evils like caste biases but urban India doesn't. Urban need to develop as urban and rural need to develop as rural. And neither need to be taxed for other's evils. We will talk more about this in the chapter around taxation, farming, reservations and others.

Chapter 3

Freedom

Democracy and freedom are an oversold or wrongly sold concept. Freedom in the form that it's been sold often leads to chaos, anarchy and unworkability. Freedom in its true sense should be something that makes your life easier. Human beings live in a social structure. At the onset, there is nothing called as freedom since you live in a co-dependent structure. The minutest of your actions and/or inactions have an impact on people and the surroundings around you. It is not something that bounds you into multiple obligations but it certainly forces you to make realizations about others' life to the extent that it constraints yours.

Freedom is a free social structure, wherein there is equal respect for an individual as well as a community's right to act without restraints. India is a free state. According to our constitution, the citizens are endowed with 'Fundamental Rights' namely freedom of expression, freedom of religion so on and so forth. But how free are we? And how much freedom should one expect from a state machinery.

In the simplest of terms, freedom is a free state of mind. However, speaking from a government point of view, complete freedom of an individual can lead to a state of chaos, thereby hindering or restricting freedom of others. This is where it gets complicated. We have been fed a notion of freedom for years to the extent that we have internalized its meaning and definition (thanks to our education system). Have we spent time thinking about and realizing its actual essence?

You might have known since your childhood that freedom of speech is being able to speak your mind, but is it really? As Voltaire so eloquently put,

Freedom translates to "I don't agree with you but I will defend to death your right to say it"

Free speech is acknowledging a man whose words make your blood boil, who's standing centre stage and advocating at the top of his lungs that which you would spend a lifetime opposing at the top of yours. *(The American President: Movie)*

Our freedom is a set of rules that bounds us to tolerate the intolerant.

> *"India is being turned intolerant. We have been much too tolerant with the intolerance. This has to end. So what should we do as citizens of India to support freedom and liberty? We should not tolerate the intolerance that undermines our democracy,"* says Amartya Sen

This was written in the light of the Dadri Lynching. How a small group has taken upon themselves to create rules and regulations in the name of 'religious sentiments' and impose them on the society at large, not only curbing their sense of freedom but also instilling in them a sense of threat in case the same is not followed. With the history of colonial rule at our backs, says Sen, we have a long and deeply etched tradition of tolerance. This being said, there has always been a streak of intolerance.

Karl Popper, the Australian philosopher, talks about the 'Paradox of tolerance' in *The Open Society and its Enemies* that, tolerance towards intolerance results in the destruction of the notion of tolerance in the society. This paradoxical state is created as the intolerant 'group' has destroyed the tolerant but tolerance as a notion also gets destroyed with them.

The need of the hour is a better freedom policy which (for example) professes freedom to no religion vs. freedom of religion. People curb other's freedom in the name of their freedom. Be it Kawar Yatra or the time of Namaz or a Christmas/Easter Procession.

Why?

It is because the only person who is not part of a mob is the person who has no time for being part of a mob. It is the one who wants to work, earn (not just money) and live well.

It is time this person says (without turning into a mob of course) – it is my movement that is curtailed due to road congestion, it is me who is late to work because of the same, it is me who gets harassed and troubled at the end of it.

Why is it acceptable for my freedom to be affected with other's freedom of religion or freedom of other basic rights? Isn't freedom of religion force feeding not only the minorities but even the majorities? Isn't this, then a flawed state of affairs?

Freedom to no religion essentially means that an individual gets to practise the religion of his/her choice, but others do not necessarily have the obligation to live with your choice of religion.

This is what is wrong with the beef ban. Taking ownership and dictating what to eat and what not to in the name of 'hurting THEIR religious sentiments'. How can someone's personal eating habits affect someone else's sentiments. Amartya Sen adds to the debate saying, "Murders have occurred on grounds of hurt sentiments from other people's private eating. Children have been denied the nourishment of eggs in school meals in parts of India for the priority of vegetarian sentiments of powerful groups."

> *"The realm of delicate sentiments seeks to extend amazingly far. They are eating at their home and your sentiments are being hurt at your home,"* Sen said sarcastically.

How should we, as a nation, go forward from here? What should be done to ensure freedom of our citizens?

The only governmental solution is creation of a Unified Civil Code (UCC), a set of rules that are basic human rules, making it mandatory for everyone to follow. Incorporating topics, which till date remain to be problematic areas for the country leading to chaos and infringement of freedom for masses. Some such topics pertain to religion, gender, caste, class so on and so forth.

The only individual solution is Moderatism. We need to change what we bring up our kids and our generations to follow against. The current world needs more celebration of moderatism. People who are happy to achieve some and want peaceful co-existence. This is perhaps what freedom of masses means from the point of view of the state machinery.

We need to teach the coming generations how all that the wars of the centuries have done is help us mature as humans and taught us the values of no-war. How every law that we follow, every scientific, religious and cultural belief that we have, are there only to bind people together and make our living as humans comfortable, and not to separate people. How freedom should actually be free and following our 'free will' should not come with compromises or threat from influential groups and/or their perspective.

While these sentiments were penned down in a pre-covid world, Coronavirus has just shown the practical implications of it. The power wielded by the governments and the curbing of freedom across continents and across communities has shown us how little it takes for us to give up our freedom, for which countries like India, The United States and multiple others have laid down hundreds of years and thousands of lives.

I don't agree with the governments approach and the subsequent lockdowns, however, what disappointed me the most was how easily people were willing to accept the fear and give up the freedom. Did any one of them really get the safety they wanted? I contracted Corona and survived, purely because it was natural selection. All the lockdowns and the vaccines of the world are not going to do much.

NEVER GIVE AWAY YOUR FREEDOM, NO MATTER WHAT.

Freedom cannot survive in vacuum. One man's freedom cannot be another man's obligation. Our social structures are primary and must rule all freedom.

Chapter 4

10 Year Road Map to End Reservations

Let's begin this chapter with a case study, a hypothetical one (obviously)

A boy comes under reservation (I would not differentiate if he is an OBC or SC or ST or a religious minority or some other reason to be differentiated)

He gets admission in a school through his reservation quota.

He grows up and completes his high school. Now he wants to pursue higher education. He applies at a university under his quota. Even though his score was less than what a general candidate who studied with him during school would require, because of reservation he gets admission in the college. After completing his graduation, he wants to expand his knowledge base even more and decides to pursue a post-graduation in his stream of choice. He applies for the course under his quota and gets the seat.

After two years, he decides that it's time to get a job and stand on his feet. So, he applies for a government job and gets it – through reservations of-course! And then gets married, has a kid and the cycle of reservation continues.

Yes, there was oppression. Yes, there was injustice. Yes, there is a need for providing stimulus for these people to catch up. But, 70 years? This is the holy grail of India's inability to develop. At some point, reservations create bums (not equality).

Bhimrao Ambedkar commented in his famous "Grammar of Anarchy" speech while introducing the constitution "In politics, we will have equality and in social and economic life we will have inequality. In politics we will be recognizing the principle of one man one vote and one vote one value. In our social and economic life, we shall, by reason of our social and economic structure, continue to deny the principle of one man one value. How long shall we continue to live this life of contradictions? How long shall we continue to deny equality in our social and economic life? If we continue to deny it for long, we will do so only by putting our political democracy in peril. We must remove this contradiction at the earliest possible moment or else those who suffer from inequality will blow up the structure of political democracy."

I say its time! This is something that over the period of time has created a rift between the so called reserved and the general 'categories'. If we have to go in flashback to give a brief of how, where and when this was started, there are several social and political affiliations of that time that we would have to consider. The varna system of 200BC which was supposed to divide people on the basis of their 'karma' or work, soon got exploited by the upper class to start division on the basis of karma. This led to grave social discrimination and oppressions such as untouchability and slavery. By the time India achieved independence, there was a need where some people, who got discriminated based on caste, class or religion, needed some policy to help them get equal participation.

But now, after 71 years of independence, do we still need it?

The question just remains, what do you want to do? Do you want to teach a man to catch fish so that he can support himself or do you want to catch a fish and give it to him everyday? Reservation is nothing but giving the fish. Neither will the man ever learn to catch a fish, given it is served to him on a platter. In my viewpoint, the politico uses this inability of them to catch a fish as a means of always keeping them down and using them as vote banks. We need someone strong to be strong and act strong!

The OBCs, according to research, are almost at par with other social groups (read upper castes) on several parameters. For instance, the OBCs are almost at par with upper castes in terms of composition of rural incomes and are investing much more than the latter in agriculture. This leads to outright misuse of a policy, which was created to provide opportunities to the communities that lag behind.

Our socio-economic and political factors clearly indicate that the reservation factor creates a defect in the policy formation of our country. In 1975, in the

State of Kerala vs N. M. Thomas Case the term 'creamy layer' in the context of reservations was coined. The judge remarked that the top of the cream layer of the reserved class will "snatch away" the reservation, while the weakest of the weak will be left as they help themselves to the crumbles of the leftover cake. Over the years, we have seen this comment turning true in oh- so many scenarios.

Does reservation really fulfil the intent for which it was first created, or has the Mandala committee's ruling been able to transpire its objective?

In a country which is already a melt point of diversity, reservations should not be the reason for sketching differences. Let's envision a caste-free India, where identities are not marked by communities or religion or caste. It could be a major stepping stone in curating what equality means for a nation.

Though the idea seems utopian, it is not altogether impossible- be it socially, economically or politically, that a practice as old as reservation can be ended instantaneously. We can, however, at least etch a roadmap with a timeline, say ten years, to put a full stop on the practice of reservation.

This again, as discussed in Chapter 1, will have to be drafted differently for the three different divisions. The solutions ought to vary from an urban resident to a semi-urban resident to a rural resident.

Let's start with the number of times one can use a quota or a reserved seat. The number of the time being more for someone living in rural, then semi-urban and finally urban (number of times decreasing in the same order). A limit can be curated which determines the number of times an individual avails reservation vs the time the individual's family avails the same. This should also keep reducing with time so that reservation exorcises by the time we reach the end of our ten-year roadmap.

The most important factor that will play a crucial role in the execution and success rate of this ten-year road map is to shed our implicit bias and hence, become debiased. Implicit social cognition or as we mentioned, implicit bias, is a phenomenon where we 'implicitly' have a bias towards a person, group or a community. This subconsciously make us associate stereotypes or preconceived notion about them. Once we as the nation's responsible citizens strip ourselves of our implicit bias and not look down at the reserved communities with pity or resentment or as unequals is when we would've made real progress.

Chapter 5

Anti- corruption

"Corruption is authority plus monopoly minus transparency."

Let me start by an assertion that goes against a lot of accepted norms, "Corruption at its base is not really bad for the development and growth of the country. However, uncontrolled corruption and no fear of corruption are evils that need to be eradicated."

Our problem as a country is not the presence of corruption, it's the pervasiveness of corruption that hurts us. It's not the traffic-cop taking bribe when they catch us breaking rules, it's the traffic-cop harassing us to get money even when we haven't broken any rules. It's the inability of people wanting to do the right thing to be able to do the right thing and live well. That's the corruption that differentiates us from some of the western countries.

Corruption for the purposes of positive development sometimes not only boosts a specific development initiative, it enables a longer-term economic growth. A perfect example of this will be what is best known as the 2G scam. I will assert that in the absence of the allocation being given the way it was, the telecom growth would have taken many years more than it did for being as pervasive as it is. The fact that telecom providers got a lot for free meant they could dole it out much cheaper. Not really planned that way, but that's how it turned out. Of course, it doesn't mean we should let go the guilty. They should be punished and fear of God should be instilled in all. If anti-corruption police stalls all development and all initiatives in the name of removing corruption, it may end up being counter-productive a.k.a the Arvind Kejriwal effect.

According to a Forbes report, every seven in ten pay bribe to access public services in India. This has become the way of life for many individuals living in the country. The fact remains that India is one of the most corrupt countries in the continent. It ranks 86th out of 180 countries. But that's just a number, written on a piece of yet another report. It's you and I who experience this corruption, the common man, the business man, the employed citizen, we all experience and live corruption everyday. Whether we like it or not we are a part of this wheel, and in order to survive, we have to turn the wheel and make it revolve. This is the explanation that most of the people give to justify their contribution to corruption. Both the rich and the poor contribute to corruption.

Why?

Social order

The social order, the so called 'system', includes groups, institutions, businesses, corporates, organizations and individuals. Given it is just almost impossible to get even a petty administrative work without some *'chai pani'*, people HAVE to participate in the cycle of corruption.

Well, it's time that we break the wheel! Even though this outrightly sounds utopian, a step by step road map to corruption free India akin to a timeline can be charted.

Before starting to decode the obvious but rampant plague of corruption, let's give a thought to the various factors around corruption. Namely, why is it important to be dealt with, how and why corruption exists in the first place and how it has slipped under the skin to the extent of being normalized.

Why corruption?

When corruption is such a villain, why at all does it exist? Well, Soutik Biswas, (in India's 'Season Of Scams.' " BBC News Soutik Biswas's India) very aptly answers this question. He says "Corruption is the only route to wealth and power." I would like to interject here and make it very clear that we aren't talking of nation's wealth and/or power here (that we will discuss in the next segment of this chapter). Corruption is the factor which makes it possible for the rich to get richer and poor to get poor. Biswas then adds "It possibly begins with the symbiotic relationship between the corruption of the poor and the corruption of the rich". The dichotomy of power and money alone has the ability to take on the economies of the world. Somewhere power buys money while somewhere else money buys power, at the end, it is the country that gets sold.

Economic growth of the country

A lot of you must be thinking that when we said corruption is the direct route to power and money, that should mean that country is prospering/ gaining. If this statement is true, then relevantly corruption should not be bad for the country.

Let's discuss this in detail, shall we?

Corruption, inequality and politics are reciprocally related when we come to talk about the economic growth of the country. It makes all the efforts towards poverty-elevation redundant. The rich get richer and the poor get poorer while the middle-class personnel remain caught up as a participant (consensual or not) in the loop of so called 'buyer' and 'seller' of the corruption marketplace. As the rate of corruption increases, It increases inequality which in turn forces people to resort to politics (Either by being the change or by being the force behind the change). Most of the time this hot blood condenses into the election of a 'populist' leader (politician) and that's how the entire revolution dies out as the elected leader now becomes the focal point of corruption.

This turns into a dangerous cycle, where in order to combat corruption people elect populist leaders and those leaders instead of tackling the problem of social inequality and corruption end up excluding the people who need the most help. Populist politics becomes elitist politics where those in power control levels of accountability and reduce transparency ("Corruption And Inequality: How Populists Mislead People")

Corruption is like cancer that destroys the economical growth of a country. United Nations curated 17 goals under Sustainable Development agenda which are to be achieved by 2030 according to the United Nation's Millennium Goals (2015). Goal number 16 states "substantially reduce corruption and bribery in all their forms" ("Peace, Justice and Strong Institutions") among other objectives.

This is because corruption increases the poverty rate, deters foreign investment, hinders economic growth and hence in turn creates an unhealthy state of affair for the country.

Transparency: Actual vs Perceived corruption

It is without a doubt that a number of surveys circulate giving us data, facts and statistics around data. They remain to be quoted and form a base for a number of theories and written pieces. While these surveys are ought to be concrete facts, they, however, remain to be highly 'subjective.'

It is impractical and almost impossible to gather ground data given the size and demographics of the country. The data actually is curated as perceived by the "business people and country experts", which has hamstrung the index from telling the entire story on corruption. Hence, these surveys are based on the opinions that can be highly biased and data that can be inaccurate.

Perceived corruption, as measured by such indexes, is lower in economically developed, long-established liberal democracies, with a free and widely read press, a high share of women in the government and a history of openness to trade. It is higher in countries that depend on fuel exports or have intrusive business regulations and unpredictable inflation. These factors explain up to 90 percent of the cross-national variation. However, measures of actual corruption experiences (based on surveys that ask businessmen and citizens in different countries whether they have been expected to pay bribes recently) correlate with hardly any of these factors once one controls for income (Daniel Treisman in his Cross National Empirical Research on Corruption).

It somehow gets highly ironic that a survey index on corruption is curated through the factors which themselves contribute to corruption.

Scale of corruption

Norm of reciprocity or 'returning favours' is a phrase that is deeply ingrained in the human psychology. We listen, exercise and implement it on a day to day basis. With the fear of missing out, the reciprocity becomes an essential phenomenon to co-exist in the society, to form an association and in turn benefit from it.

With corruption rampant to the extent of being a normalized everyday phenomenon, the norm of reciprocity is glued hard to it. While people practice and/or participate in corruption by overstepping or ignoring the ethical code, they somewhere feel that it is their moral obligation to reciprocate the favour taken. The irony here is just unparalleled.

And what does favour for a favour, wait! Let me rephrase. What does bribe for a bribe do? It makes the whole nation corrupt.

What can be done?

Let's start with a liberalist approach given eradicating corruption is not a fortnight phenomenon. A liberalist point of view would strip the burden off of corruption and point out that corruption at the highest level, specially corruption that leads to positive development doesn't hurt anyone. Let's take the example of 2G. In reality (may be in hindsight), the entire Indian economic growth in the 21st century was caused by the explosion and the reduced costs of telecom. These reduced costs were enabled by the corruption in the 2G allocation, which enabled the telecom providers to service so economically and hence spur the overall growth.

I know you would be raising an eyebrow, but this is the ideal way to tackle the problem of corruption- by looking at the larger picture in the context of country's development. We should start with removing corruption for the SMEs. Given that starting at a small scale is more practical, start with the lowest level where it ceases to trouble the lower-middle class.

Powerful and growth oriented SMEs are the key to success. They provide higher employment, they provide opportunities and they enable economic growth at the highest level.

GOVERNMENT

Chapter 6

Minimize Governance

Let us, for the convenience of this chapter, establish the concept of 'market' in the context of the prosperity of a country as a rhetoric. Like any individual needs to earn for his living and survival, a country too needs to create a system of market, which creates a standard of living for the society, creates employment opportunities, and overall generates 'wealth' for the country. (We are using the word 'wealth' in its loose form). But this is no rocket science, we all know that money is important, be it for a person or for the state.

Government has never been a positive enabler of change and development anywhere in the world. The best the government can do is to minimize and reduce its involvement and let the forces of nature and the market take over. The advent of digital has made it even truer. Just like judiciary is kept separate from the executive to ensure justice, similarly government interference or participation should be kept minimum for a healthy economical state of affair.

The Modi government of 2014 & 2019 came with a lot of promise in this area. However, as someone aptly put, before the Modi government the government in India was all over in business's pants, post the Modi government the government in India has gotten into people's shorts. Not the right development structure.

The concept of free market is not a new one. There are avid number of case studies and examples that show the success of the model. Even a mixed model with a regulatory government at the top level is a negotiable structure. Such a model not only enables a business-friendly environment, it also creates a space for employment opportunities.

In such a structure:

- The government does not intervene in the economic decisions of the companies/organizations/firms
- Entrepreneurs are free to bring in/setup business in any sector, thereby developing infrastructure, technology and access to world export
- Consumers are at the receiving end as they benefit from low prices.

Singapore, is the ideal example to practise the model and holds a GDP of US $349.7 billion (2018). Quoting from the passages of a Bloomberg report.

> *"In Singapore, civil-servant bonuses rise and fall with the economy's performance... The nation...links civil servants' bonuses to how well the $298 billion economy does. ...Civil servants are typically paid a variable incentive twice a year, on top of a fixed one-month bonus. The mid-year payment was skipped in 2009, when the economy contracted during the global recession... "Singapore may be one of the few countries that explicitly pegs bonuses to growth,"* said Vishnu Varathan, an economist in Singapore at Mizuho Bank Ltd."

Now that's a smart way to boost economy and curb corruption, both at the same time. Okay, let's put the analysis in place. Singapore does not really have any natural resources, apart from ocean access. So obviously its spectacular economic performance has to be credited to the country's good economical policy. The corporate tax is as low as 17% and the government spending is extremely small when compared to the global standards. The investment and labour freedom makes the country rank 2nd in the economic freedom score out of 42 countries in Asia Pacific.

While we are quoting the benefits of the free market economy system, we are not saying to take the model as it is and copy paste like a plagiarized page. There are always two sides to the same coin and hence we cannot altogether be neglecting the negative consequences of the model. While this structure can prove to be pro-business economy, will it work in a country like India? We are aware that in a country like ours a free market economy system can end up being precarious for the people who lack the agency of being competitive. With our literacy levels not being at par, this model will need some work on our parts.

Some basic guidelines and regulations are ought to be placed by the government to keep things in check. Taking heed from our previous chapter on reservation, strategies such as use of a policy favouring less abled can be put in place, **with specified number of times** that the policy can be used.

Many people argue that despite the fact that Singapore functions on a free market economy model, the government has an important role to play. Given the small domestic paradigm of the country, it is ought to be open to international opportunities. This by the way, if not already assumed, makes the country vulnerable. It is here where the government of Singapore has an important aspect to play. While it provides a business friendly environment, it does not itself abstain from participating. According to statistics, almost 22% of GDP comes from govt. sector.

In a developing country like India, a free market with regulatory government is the mechanism for growth. Prosperity happens not by restricting growth, prosperity happens when free market is allowed to provide economic growth.

Caution to the wind must be thrown while minimizing governance. Coronavirus has again showed us how ineffective the corporate and the capitalist structure is in cases of crisis. Corporate greed and the need for incessant leveraging takes over sanity and prudent planning. The ones that may not leverage themselves well are called ineffective and punished badly by the stock market hawks. We saw this in full blood in 2008 as well. So, while minimizing governance is absolutely the need, some top level regulatory has to maintain the balance.

GST
28%
18%
12%
5%
SATISH ACHARYA

Chapter 7

Refine Tax Structure

We, the Indians, either pay too much taxes or not at all. It's an extremely dangerous situation. While there have been numerous reforms over the years, its still a huge problem. The answer lies in increasing the number of people that come under the ambit of tax payers, significantly reducing the amount of money the government requires to run the government and decreasing the tax rates.

Started with the aim to maintain wealth distribution in the country, taxes have taken a negative connotation in the past few decades. Given the baggage of corruption that the term carries, taxes have been seen government's way to embezzle money from the common man.

Carrying forward the conversation initiated in the previous chapters, government's association needs to be minimized to strip off its claim on the people's money in the form of taxes. People need to see the meaning of taxes in its truest form and thereby deduce the importance it has for the economic stability of the country.

It is without a doubt that taxation has an influence on the economical trends of the country. It is said to believe that multinational firms access a country for investment or distribution of profits on the level of the country's taxation. But it is important to take into consideration the political and historically infused trajectory that tax reforms go through.

Talking about India, given the socio-economical and historical background that our country has, it is bound to have traversed a long path of constant evolution. The most important aspect of the Indian taxation system, which still acts as the backbone of the entire framework, was added at the time of independence. It was the division of taxes between the Centre and the States. It was started as the means to transfer private funds for public consumption and investment (Bagchi and Stern, 1994).

The evolution of tax policy within the framework of public sector based, heavy industry dominated, import substituting industrialisation strategy has had several implications. First, tax policy was directed to raise resources for large and increasing requirements of public consumption and investment irrespective of the efficiency implications it entailed. Second, the objective of achieving socialistic pattern of society on the one hand and the large oligopolistic rents generated by the system of licences, quotas and restrictions on the other, necessitated steeply progressive tax structure in both direct and indirect taxes. Third, pursuit of multiplicity of objectives enormously complicated the tax system with adverse consequences on efficiency and horizontal equity. This also opened up large avenues for evasion and avoidance of taxes. The disregard for efficiency considerations was a part of import substituting industrialisation strategy. Fourth, all of the above required not only differentiation in tax rates based on arbitrary criteria but also legitimised selectivity and discretion in tax policy and administration. This gained legitimacy from the plan priorities. Once selectivity and discretion were accepted as legitimate, it mattered little whether these were exercised as intended. This provided enough scope for the special interest groups to influence tax policy and administration. Fifth, the influence of special interest groups, changing priorities and lack of information system and scientific analysis led to ad hoc and often, inconsistent calibration of policies. Finally, poor information system was both the cause of selective application of the tax system as well as its effect. (Rao, M and Rao, R, 2012: Trends & Issues in Tax Policy and Reform in India)

Now, tax is as important as the minister on the economical chess board of a country. According to the World Bank, the economic performance of developing countries has a direct co-relation with the country's taxation policies.

With our backdrop firm and grounded, we have to say it out loud that India's tax policy needs some major reforms.

Why?

Let's see some facts*

- According to the December 2017 report of the income-tax department, only 1.6% of Indians pay income tax.

- Even the relatively incentive-compatible goods and services tax (GST) is fraught with high compliance costs, too many rates and classifications.
- Taxes on consumption tend to be regressive, because poor people spend a greater proportion of their income on consumption—and consumption is taxed at high rates in India.

It is no hidden fact that people with association and wealth have found a way to rid themselves off of tax paying. Arun Jaitley made it pretty evident that there lies a large gap between the tax collection and income/consumption pattern.

Let's talk about GST, shall we?

Good and services tax (GST) was proposed as a ray of hope, a modern and transparent indirect tax system, was supposed to be the best tax reform since country's independence. It failed to comply with its famous 'one nation, one market, one tax' policy which was actually the crux of the entire reform itself. Consumption is taxed at a higher rate, even though most of the Indian population has consumption based income. And what is with the tax division on items? While gold is taxed at 3%, everyday items such as biscuits are taxed at 18%.

Given that the GST structure is, but, simplification of the tax system, wasn't it supposed to reduce the number of people employed by the central and the state tax department? Creating more structures and making things more complicated, has perhaps been the worst policy of all times.

The need of the hour is to define and redefine tax structures. The image of the tax collector needs to change from a conniving thief to humble public servant. Establishment of belief if not trust is the first step towards healthy tax system and dealing with anti-corruption goes hand in hand (the same will be discussed in the following chapters).

Better structured tax slabs will automatically lead to an increase in the percentage of people paying taxes. While stringent action should be taken against those who do not comply. This is not an overnight activity, but at least a roadmap can be curated which eventually helps in achieving the objective of taxation.

TAX
SPEND

Chapter 8

Accountability to the taxpayer

The fundamental complaint from most people against the Indian tax system is that they don't see their taxes being used for their benefit. And this notion is not completely flawed. The reality of our system is that the tax payer and the tax benefiter are different. There is a small set of people in this country that pays taxes and most of those taxes get used up for a completely different set of people.

When it comes to taxpaying, there have been plenty of examples (as mentioned in the previous chapters) which show that there is huge disparity between the people who are supposed to pay tax (as per the statistics) vs. the people who actually pay tax. While all we question are the tax payer's intent and deceit, why does nobody question the tax collector?

The Income Tax Act, 1961, jots down compliances for the tax payers. The penalties and consequences are defined incase the tax payer violates any tax provision. However, there are no guidelines/provisions/consequences laid out for tax collectors and we will not be wrong in saying that the same has been misused at the expense of taxpayers. This in turn, has created an environment of distrust and zero accountability. While it doesn't justify the problem, but it wouldn't be wrong to say that this is perhaps one of the key reasons for people not wanting to pay taxes.

The police department in Los Angeles gets paid from the city tax collected. Now that is some ownership on the tax collector's part. This, then ensures 100% accountability on the part of the police department.

What is it exactly that the taxpayer is paying for? The tax collectors are endowed with huge discretionary powers which makes the department unaccountable. The relationship between accountability and tax must consider that what can be organized for the public and where will the capacity to do so rest. Public accountability in India has become non-existent.

Importance of public accountability

Public accountability is the cornerstone for public services. When the public is aware and informed, they form the thread in helping the country move forward. Even with a hierarchical organizational fabric, a legal nudge is not sufficient to ensure that seamless flow of public accountability. There remains a need for the coherent interaction between the two ends of the pole- namely, the taxpayer and the tax collector. For an external accountability to function, there needs to be an emotion of internal responsibility present. As neither can function without each other. Aristotle was the first philosopher who tried to connect the two factors for a seamless public functioning in affairs in an administrative set up. According to him 'virtues, such as justice, practical wisdom, truthfulness and liberality, are significant elements in order to balance external and internal features of the organisations'. While we do agree that these are hardcore virtues if we translate them into reality. Hence, we'd render it to be utopian but it does not negate the essentiality of the same.

'Governments exist to satisfy the needs of their citizens' and rightly so, governments are elected to 'put their citizens first'. And the prospects of accountability have more grave repercussions than just moral obligations. When a question of liability starts hanging in a democracy, it starts to become a barrier in the political, social as well as economic progress.

State of affairs

We have a federal setup and the above doctrine of bilateral affairs between the public and the officials cannot be more true and effective. For explanation sake let's just call it upward accountability and downward accountability respectively. Upward accountability comes through the government in implementation of the various legal obligations whereas downward accountability is to the public.

> *"Indian democracy is functioning in a society where extreme social and economic inequality exists in its defining feature. The Indian society is deeply divided socially and economically in terms of caste, class, gender, rural-urban and regional inequalities."*

> *"India is indeed a vibrant democracy but it is increasingly showing the signs of a dysfunctional democracy, where the institutions of democracy are not serving the interests of all the people. They are being controlled and manipulated by the ruling elite."* (C. Rammanohar Reddy, Editor of The Economic)

Public has a right to know where their resources, collected in the form of taxes, are utilized. Transparency is the key for a holistic development. It is for the law makers of the country to ensure this visibility towards the citizens. Be it through stringent application of provisions for tax payers or creation of new ones to reduce corruption at the hands of the tax collectors.

"The arbitrary exercise of power by state, the flouting of the rule of the law by agencies of the state and protection of the rich and powerful from the law are the three unhealthy features of the Indian democracy," said the ET editor C Rammanohar Reddy in an event. And this is exactly what we need to overcome.

The above factors are the reason that there remains an inherent lack of faith on the part of the citizens. This void is what creates a feeling of retaliation amongst the citizens and hence we witness a number of tax defaults. There needs to be a system where people come to terms with the way their resources are utilized so that they become an active participant in the development of the country.

> *"The law sometimes can be written in such subjective manner that it affects the efficiency and transparent functioning of the government. If the statute provides for pointless discretion to agency, it is in essence demolishing the accountability strand within the administrative process, as the agency is not under obligation from an objective norm, which can enforce accountability in the decision-making process. All law making, be it in the context of delegated legislation or primary legislation,*

have to conform to the fundamental tenets of transparency and openness on the one hand and responsiveness and accountability on the other. These are fundamental tenets flowing from due process requirement under Article 21, equal protection clause embodied in Article 14, and fundamental freedoms ingrained in Article 19. A modern deliberative democracy cannot function without these attributes." (Global Energy Ltd. vs Central Electricity Regulatory Commission: supreme court verdict*)*

Firing a government employee for non-performance is must have. It's not anti-socialist.

Chapter 9

Refine Elections

Elections are essential for a true democracy to work and function the way a democracy should. But when elections and their subsequent campaign and not governance become the end goal, the crux of being a democracy is lost. With 29 state elections, one national election every 5 years averages to around 1 election every 2.5 months, India is a 'high-on-election zone'. And this does not even include the innumerable Vidhan Sabha elections, Zilla Parishad elections, Panchayat elections, and municipal elections throughout the year. We live in an environment where the politicians of the country are always campaigning and always fighting elections. What scope of development does that leave us with? Does anybody even think of development or its just relentless running in a useless rat race? How do the citizens of the country feel about it and what do they take away from it?

While all the above rhetorical questions speak for themselves, there is a loud cry for refinement when it comes to our election system.

Simultaneous elections

Simultaneous elections or 'one nation, one election' is a conversation that has been making rounds for some time now. There have been pointers raised as to why and how it is good or bad for the nation. We strongly agree that simultaneous elections as a concept is a great idea, given that it gets executed well. Not only will it help bring down the cost and human labour associated with elections, it will also put a stop to this Sisyphean circle of politicians always competing and shunning each other down. It has the capability of ushering us into an era of constructive developments, reforms and yes even constructive competitions and elections.

Talk about curbing corruption, isn't this hitting two targets with one stone? It is without doubt that black money and corruption is rampant when we talk about election. We are not taking away from the efforts that election commission is putting in to fight corruption, but why not take a more comprehensive and logical approach.

Let's strive for an electoral system which does not keep revolving in the rudimentary of fighting election but actually reach the ultimate objective: Governance

Realize the vote's worth

While a democracy is about providing capability to get a government which is to the people, for the people, by the people, one obstacle in achieving this true democratic apparatus is to ensure people treat their vote with respect. Democracy has a tendency to become a system where the ones that don't know any better goes out to vote and the ones that know don't!

Is it fair to provide a vote to somebody who doesn't even understand the value his/her vote has and ends up creating worse situations? Shouldn't we look at a different process of how the government is elected by elevating the status of a vote so that it is not taken for granted? And we are not at all proposing that a person who is less literate or illiterate for that matter, takes their vote for granted, but we are actually putting forth the idea that they might not have the where with all to make a choice.

Think of a system where people who actually understand the ramification of their votes, get to exercise the activity. A system with more advanced eligibility criteria to vote than just an age limit. We are not living in 1947 anymore where the literacy level of the country is extremely low. While at the same time we are not withstanding an illiterate's right to vote, it should just be of a lesser value, say maybe contribute to half a vote than his educated counterpart. Let a vote exude the power it has and let people realize it.

While, we do agree that this proposition sounds utopian, it is time now that we start to think about the required refinements in the system that lead to the destination.

The power of decision making

One of the core pillars of the Indian democracy is the capability of executing fair voting and not necessarily election of a fair government. Well, it is not a secret that political, especially election campaigns are based on some or the other propaganda, each one of which is aimed to resonate with the audience. Propaganda has been defined as "the more or less systematic effort to manipulate other people's beliefs, attitude or reaction by means of symbols". It is created and flouted around to make the audience, the voters feel that the party is connected to them and understands their pain points. Be it regional, local, or even religion-based, every agenda is curated to instil- 'we understand you'-'we will provide you remedy'-feeling. Fear and hate have always been the most important emotions.

Data analysis is done by Psephologists at a bucket level. Before the big internet boom, the analysts collated precinct voting data, public opinion polls, campaign finance information and similar statistical data. People's opinion and point of views were noted to generate a propaganda that resonated with the voters. Ideology is created and propagated, minds are washed, votes are cast without realization, leaders misuse power and position.

While we are raising a bar when we say that people's votes should be marked and arranged according to their qualification of literacy or illiteracy, a more distinguished eligibility process should be in place for people standing for elections. Do you think it is fair that an illiterate person who does not understand the ramification of decision making gets elected just because a particular section of the society 'needs' to be represented? While no one can pre-judge how a newly formed government will fare out, we can at least ensure a system that ensures no undeserving person has the power to play with the country.

Let me give you a reference point, post the 'Monica Lewinsky' scandal, Bill Clinton was in line to be impeached. Not because he got head from an intern while sitting in the White House, but because he lied to the American people.

Can you even imagine this in India, where politicians lie all the time , and its not even frowned upon? Now, this is not to say that American Politicians are truth seekers. But, it does make the point.

A two-party system?

Indian politics centres around people forming regional entities and using these as levers to control and get favours. It is time we reform that. With a history of revolutionaries, India has a long heritage of new blood encompassed of new thought, new wave. This in turn prompted a need for a multiparty system in the country decades ago. It's a laughable thought in the current Indian political structure consisting of JDU, RJD, NCP, SP, BSP, TDP, TRS, DMK, BJD, AAP – and on and on and on.

Every political party (regional or national) need to have a vision – a vision for the development of the region that they represent. They need to forge alliances aligned to that vision. This conversion of people's votes and elected individuals into levers is killing our country. This is perhaps the top of the pyramid underneath which our mob mentality, our corruption, our biases and most of our other social evils sit.

> One election every
> 5 years, states &
> national
> combined.

बिजली हाफ, पानी माफ

Chapter 10

Popular Nationalism

The world is moving from a state of regionalism to a state of globalism. This transition in itself is remarkable. While the manifestation of this change across the world is leading to newer economies and newer social structures, it is also leading to significant pressure on the existing world order.

What we are seeing is people aggregating in their communities and seeking what they consider as their entitled privileges. Essentially, the privileged are losing their privileges in much higher modes than ever before in the history.

It is no longer popular nationalism or right wing structures as they are being talked about. They are much more intricate. It's more a voice of survival what we are hearing.

Globalism in this scenario essentially means the movement of people from one geography to other, from one social structure to other. This is putting tremendous pressure on the older structures and hence the rise of popular nationalism. As mentioned in the chapter on equality, there is a rising concern from the people with means about losing the means. This order is changing at a pace too fast. The migrants who enter into Europe (The middle east and Africa) and in America (Mexico and Latin America) and in India (from Bangladesh, Myanmar) have started to put too much pressure on the already settled communities. The increased violence, the increased breakages in the systems are giving too much reason for people to complain.

The rise of conspiracy theories keeps everybody on the edge. We talked about the spread and the pervasiveness of social media making it worse.

It is a religious or a racial war, even if that's not the case for the population in general. Let me ask the following question – if you are an Islamic leader and your job is to increase the spread of Islam in Europe and US, what will you do? You can't fight a bloody war with them, not with the disparity of resources. What you can do, however, is to get a few million people to move to Europe and US. Settle and multiply. Isn't that what we are already seeing through Syria & North Africa?

The deep-rooted agendas (like the spread of socialist / Marxist philosophies in India) are starting to come to the fore and disrupting the delicate balance. Reality is that there is a need for an equal world order, not a subsidy/reservation/ oppression based world order. An equal opportunity world order. Those who can't run will lag behind but such is the nature of humanity. Let's be human!

Why should someone who contributes through taxes, who work hard, who has earned every means he has, be okay with someone else getting freebies. That's a fundamental debate we need to resolve. All world order (regional, national, global) emerges from there.

NO FREEBIES, NO SUBSIDIES, WE ALL ARE EQUAL AND SHOULD HAVE EQUAL OPPORTUNITY AND EXCEL BASED ON WHAT WE DO WITH THE OPPORTUNITY!

Love thy country &
hate thy neighbors
are not
synonymous.

Chapter 11

Nationalize Farming

Please don't get me wrong. This chapter is consistent with my thoughts around minimize governance. The headline is just to get the reader to roll their eyes, think of all the agitations, demonstrations, mobs and everything else the farmers will do if anything in their sacred world is touched, bite their tongue knowing this line of thinking around agitations is the wrong way and its what this book has as one of its key themes and want to read on. It is about proposing some key reforms to happen in agriculture and farming, not really about nationalizing farming. If some readers want to pursue the topic of nationalizing farming, I suggest they email me at kapgup@gmail.com and I will be happy to explore this further with them.

Now back to the topic: The current political structure of our country has gone from paying people to vote before the elections (which since has been made illegal) to promising farm loan waivers post elections (currently considered legal). There is billions of dollars (literally billions) in these farm loan waivers.

The literal translation of this in my view is that farming is not a profitable business (at least in certain conditions). I have tried multiple sources and numerous experts with conflicting opinions from everywhere and hence had to give up on it, however, I can certainly confirm that this farm loan waiver is one of the top 5 evils spreading in this country, and spreading like wildfire.

First, lets acknowledge farming as an industry, not a noble profession. Yes it feeds me. But that doesn't change anything about farming as an industry (a necessary one).

Now, let's look at the reality of the situation. In most family owned businesses, the challenge is always in succession and how to grow. Most businessperson's kids over decades have either diversified into other lines of business or grown their existing businesses or some of the kids have chosen to pursue other professions. This has ensured a business created by one businessperson can take care of all their kids* or ensure all of them are able to sustain. This is perhaps the initiation point (not the complete reason of course) of where the farming issues began to get worsened. Farmers get their land as inheritance from generations and use it to earn their living. They do very little to diversify or increase the spectrum of what all they can do. Combined with other historical, cultural and social factors, we have a situation where in a large segment of our farmers are micro farmers, with unsustainable land sizes and large growing families to feed. Coupled with lack of technological know-how and an ecological balance that is making farming difficult without technology, it is resulting into a lot of farmers not being able to meet ends. This is where the real intervention needs to happen.

In all my research around farming, I have gathered that farming is a rather profitable business (much more than a lot of other industries) if the basic conditions are met. A key obstacle in agriculture and farming industry is perhaps an issue that every manufacturing industry has been facing for the last couple of decades, namely, the disparity of profit distribution between the various hands involved in an end-to-end transaction. The supply chain in farming is definitely very profitable, the question is how to simplify the process and ensure the farmer reaps some of this profit. This is where real intervention needs to happen.

In my view, moment this intervention becomes socialistic in nature, it loses its purpose. A socialistic intervention is done by a set of privileged people demonstrating their supremacy to an under-privileged class and ensuring the levers of power can be held by them. In my view, the solution need to be what any other industry would have done. Creation of a private-public structure, wherein the basic necessities and growth of the entire ecosystem can be done. This, and only this, should be the governments intervention. Any other special privileges, loan waivers, tax waivers, subsidies etc should be implemented within this private-public structure and the entire industry of farming should become a profitable venture. Interestingly, this approach is what has resulted in the entire industrial revolution, renaissance, the startup culture and the rise of new business models.

The New Farm Acts_2020 & the corresponding protests around them are a great showcase of what is wrong in the farming world. The laws by themselves make sense, however, like anything else, the devil is in the actual details of their implementation. If done well, they will eradicate a good portion of this farming middlemen and greatly benefit the industry. In my view, that is what the power players are most worried about. This single change could alter the entire course of Indian - Political, Economic & Social structure. As the COVID-19 pandemic has shown, the right food and enough food goes beyond everything else. Farming is an industry however, perhaps the most important industry which is why it should not be dealt with subsidies.

Chapter 12

The Non Socialist India

Money, the key motivating factor in society for a lot of things has been around for ages now but the concept has evolved quite a bit. From being a support system that would help you lead your life and ensure that you don't go to sleep at night to becoming a menace that is making our society's hunger increase at an exponential rate. It is a drastic change that we have come to observe in the past many years.

Earlier, people used to rule with the sheer amount of power they had, the power to influence, the power to govern and the power to understand the grievances and the situations of money. Today, governance has gotten a new twist to it. In the current scenario, the richest govern the governments and that is because money hasn't just remained to be an element of trade. Money has actually become power.

With the growing population and the growing needs for food, housing and water, resources are getting scarce whilst the population is expanding rapidly. This has created somewhat of a misbalance in society where everybody is now more concerned about the amount of money they earn not just because they want to lead a certain standard of life which is also not untrue but because they believe that financial security and holding funds for later will actually help them in the long run to sustain any setbacks that they might or might not face.

This growing need to hoard more and more money, more and more resources is exactly what has contributed to what we call today as Capitalism. The fact that everybody is out there to make a profit for themselves and is willing to let other people die in exchange of more money is what is the problem with our society today. Now you may look at capitalism differently and say that it has led to multiple advances in the society which might not have been possible otherwise. The view is not entirely wrong but it doesn't give out the full picture. It doesn't tell you the demerits that capitalism entails. Let me shower some more light upon what I am talking about.

The No. 1 demerit of capitalism is Inheritance

What kind of world are we living in where just by the virtue of your parents, your ancestors being rich, you get to keep the remains of whatever they created throughout their lifespan? It is more or less similar to when a king dies, the throne is then automatically bequeathed to his son on the behalf that the kings son is the rightful owner of this kingdom, no matter how incapable the son might be, it is his fate to govern the lives of people without being even a bit qualified for the Job.

Similarly, when you take money from dead people and give it to their children, it almost reiterates the same thing. So a kings son will always inherit so much that he will never have to work a day in his life, will always be at an advantage in respect to other people who are at a similar age, a similar stage to what he is, people who are actually smarter than him but the only thing which they lack is the right lineage.

Inheritance tells us that luck governs more of your life than your talent or dedication ever will. So we are saying that by virtue of being rich, their kids will remain rich and subsequently the upcoming generations will remain rich and the cycle will continue till the time the lineage is destroyed and the family tree is dead.

On the other hand, people who come from an underprivileged background will never get a chance to compete with the top class because they will always be low on money and no matter how much they do what they do, unless they become Bill Gates or Steve Jobs (both of which also came from money) will never be able to achieve anything substantial in life and at best, there upcoming generations will leave a middle class life. So we are saying that socialism is non existent, which it is and the only shot at having a life like the people who have had inheritances is to run into a lot of luck which is highly unlikely.

Specially in countries like India where the disparity between classes is as stark, there should be larger inheritance taxes or estate taxes to ensure some semblance of equality can be generated. If 50% of Mukesh Ambani's money can be used for the welfare of a million underprivileged kids and 50% is to be divided between his kids, they would still stand to be the richest people in India. But on the other hand, those million kids would now have a life.

I am not just talking about the Mukesh Ambani's of the world. Even people like me, people of some means should not be able to simply transfer their wealth to their coming generations.

The No. 2 demerit of Capitalism is the Stock Market

Can somebody please explain to me why the bloody thing works? How is it not just legalised gambling where you put your money only to not know whether you will end up winning or losing? Isn't it just a game of chance? If by chance Elon Musk tweeted badly about a brand, your money in it will be lost because apparently the stock market gets influenced by something as little as a tweet. Or maybe, the bigger stakeholders make such tweets and the stock market replies to them because all of it is just a big strategy to snatch money from small, ignorant investors who don't understand how the world works.

For me, stock market is a classical case of rich getting richer and hence need to be dealt with.

Should the stock market simply be shut down or a minimum investment timeframe be defined (maybe a month) or some other criterion that ensures business are able to raise money when they need it whilst not becoming a gambling pot? Most investors may be listening to other experts and think of themselves as analysts but really, the fluctuation in the stock market, doesn't it seem like mood swings?

The No. 3 demerit of Capitalism is Interest rate

Rich getting richer while poor suffers – this is considered a key evil in the society. This is what keeps us from providing equality. But what's the cause?

The constitution declares India to be a sovereign, socialist, secular, democratic republic. But we have done little to achieve a better socialist society. Socialism here means equal opportunity, equal rights and equal ability to be able to live well, NOT equal pay. It is equal pay based on work done irrespective of all other factors.

If looked closely, socialism would essentially mean that rich shouldn't be able to get richer just by the virtue of being rich and because we as a society provide equality. However, India, as an economy, suffers from an extremely high interest rate problem. A high interest rate means rich can live out of just being able to lend money and earn more. Money attracts money. It also makes it more difficult for businesses to flourish and makes entrepreneurship more difficult.

One key change I expect to see in the Indian economy in the next few years is a marked reduction in interest rates. At least a 2-3% reduction! In itself, this is the most socialist of changes that the country will see.

Interestingly, lower interest rates would also support a real estate sector in need of support. Every 1% reduction in interest rate will increase real estate rates by at-least 3-5%.

So, better real estate, increased entrepreneurship, lower inflation. What more can you ask for?

Unregulated socialism or unmanaged capitalism. Both disasters waiting to happen.

Chapter 13

Martyrdom versus Success

Take the fantasy, mythology and aspects of historical significance out, our reality history as an Indian starts with infidelity and treachery of some of its own people. In the invasion of Sind by Mahommed-Bin-Kasim, the military commanders of King Dahar accepted bribes from the agents of Mahommed-Bin-Kasim and refused to fight on the side of their King. Jaichand invited Mahommed Gohri to invade India and fight against Prithvi Raj with the help of the Solanki Kings. The Maratha noblemen and the Rajput Kings fought for the Moghul Emperors when Shivaji was fighting for the liberation of Hindus. Gulab Singh, the principal commander of the Sikh kingdom let the British destroy the Sikh Rulers. The Sikhs refused to participate in the first Indian mutiny of 1857. And the partition of 1947, the creation of India, Pakistan and East Pakistan (now known as Bangladesh) puts the icing on the cake.

To add to this, our freedom struggle taught us the value of martyrdom. The history we are taught is not of INA (Indian National Army) and its contribution to our freedom; the history we are taught is the lines and lines of Indian's being beaten up by British and for them to never stand down and that stoic behaviour getting us our independence. The story we are taught is not of someone who won something, but someone who gave their life for something.

This is part of the DNA that we as Indians have inherited. For us, success comes only with treachery and corrupt behaviour. We don't believe people can succeed without doing wrong. And we look at all success with this scepticism, we look at all successful people with the same amount of disdain. Our love for the Anna Hazares of the world stems from this.

While this disdain and this scepticism is not unfounded, the world is shifting around us. And herein lies the need for us to shift as well. As discussed in the chapter on equality, it is the measure of number of lifetimes it takes for a person of ability to make it from bottom to the top. This success needs to be recognized and celebrated. It should be looked upon in the view of the effort, the hard work, the sacrifices that went in to create that success. It shouldn't be looked in terms of the moral analysis of the person or the person's life.

Let us relook at the social structure of life overall. There are the Alphas (people who are on top and they feed on the ability for them to be on top and for people to follow them). Then there are the Betas (people who to date are good followers). All our quest as humanity (from women empowerment to reservations to globalization) has been built on the rationale of moving people from Betas to Alphas. However, the need is for creating a third social entity, I call it as Gamma. These are people who strive on a basic slogan, live and let live. They want to look at their life and its pursuits, they want to keep moving ahead, they are fiercely competitive, but they don't need people following them. They are the lone-wolfs. Our education system needs to strive towards making more gammas. This is the aspect of moderatism we talked about in freedom.

For me, moderatism means happiness. Happiness or the ability to enjoy life as it comes is a blessing that I have simply come to enjoy. Here are a few simple hacks to practice moderatism that I have used and perfected over the years to:

- Whenever angry, just turn away and smile. I am not asking you to remember a funny situation or do anything crazy, just spread your lips and put a smile on your face
- Breathe in & breathe out 3 times, whenever faced with anything you don't like
- Do not (and I mean it) worry about what people do or how people contribute or take away from their life. That is their life and their way of living. Have no expectations and fulfil no expectations. Just do what you think is right

Do this well for a bit and it will start coming naturally to you. And then, invincible you will be. Not because you will be a great warrior, rather because there will be nothing to win from you.

Chapter 14

Women Empowerment

The name of the game is equality. In the 21st century, we can't be talking about biases. Gender, race, sexual orientation, caste or anything else, the name of the game is equality. Equality of opportunity, Equality that ensures everyone has equal rights to grow. However, for reasons of only historical importance, we are still stuck in the past. Our meaning of equality as a society is framed by reservations, privileges, special subsidies and a growing cancel culture against that.

Amongst all this, the most important is women empowerment. 50% of our race has been unequal for centuries, that certainly is a matter of concern. However, we can't change that. Some of us may consider that history as oppression, others may consider it as requirement. I consider it as history, a social order prevalent at that point of time. A social order that doesn't work in our current society. A social order that must be changed.

I don't want to talk about the generics of women empowerment, we all know that. Firstly, in my view, the biggest obstacle to women empowerment is the women themselves. Every empowered women need to stand on the sidelines and support other women to grow. Instead, most women however empowered continue to play the women card to get ahead. I think that derails the issue of women empowerment to a huge degree in all aspects of life. This one issue for me is a global problem. Think about people like Meghan Markle or Oprah who still claim to be victims and oppressed.

Secondly, the world is not made equal. There is not going to be any 2 people irrespective of their gender who would be leading equal lives, earning equal money, facing equal problems etcetera etcetera. The permutation combinations of life are such that attaining equality in a society is just near impossible. What people & feminists especially need to understand is the fact that none of us are superior or inferior to one another. Everybody has their own skills and their own life, we are only equal in the sense that none of us will ever be equal. Women empowerment could be about justifying the gap between a nurse's and an engineer's salary, it can't be about making equal number of nurses and engineers. That will be a biological anomaly. Every girl interested in becoming an engineer should become an engineer and that's equality, but promoting housewives as disempowered is as wrong as promoting house husbands as henpecked. To any feminist or advocate of women empowerment, a housewife is going to be a perfect example of how women are oppressed in the society that they have to resort to household chores as a way of life. But, there is a flip side to the coin. Have you ever even considered the fact that becoming a housewife is a conscious decision that they made? Why can they not be empowered and yet willing to make their number one priority their home? Why don't we let them decide what they want in life and get on with it? Why the pressure on every woman to fit into a mould that you feel is the indication of being progressive?

A good example for me is pregnancy. I find the maternity benefits that organizations are forced to give to women as very regressive. Is maternity a woman's decision? I think it's a family's decision. Then why doesn't the family assume responsibility for it? How many 'empowered' women say no to maternity benefits because they are empowered or because they have families that believe in equality?

On a side note, while the me too movement brought into foray the misuse and abuse of power by countless men, some of them even claiming they didn't know its wrong. I don't support any such men and any acts of indiscretion definitely needed punishment. But, I would want to understand why there hasn't been a formal apology from the women across the world who slept their way to success. The Me Too movement was great and required, it brought out the reality of how sexual favours are a commodity traded in huge numbers. While most people found it to be a revolutionary feat for women across the world because they stood up to their abusers, I would want to ask who enabled the abusers? Was it the amount of power & money they had? I would say yes if the abusee claims to be raped and was physically forced into the act but what about the ones that used it to their advantage? Did it with multiple men across the spectrum and took away opportunity from hundreds of other women, of equal or more talent but unwilling to trade their bodies for success.

The answer is never going to be women empowerment, the answer is going to be equality in a sense that as a society, we aim to provide people with the right kind of spaces that they require in order to feel safe and grow. We don't need to give the same pedestal to all the women, we need to give the right pedestals to the right women and that is the only way this society can evolve.

We can evolve this thought to all forms of equality (all forms of discrimination). We have changed as a society and using these repeated conversations about reparations or special subsidies is only going to further the gap. True equality comes from one thing and that's equality only. The initiator need to be empowered women and everyone shall follow suit.

Chapter 15

Control Social Media

It was the best of times, it was the worst of times, it was the age of wisdom, it was the age of foolishness, it was the epoch of belief, it was the epoch of incredulity, it was the season of Light, it was the season of Darkness, it was the spring of hope, it was the winter of despair.

Charles Dickens wrote these famous lines for a completely different world in a completely different time. The ability of it being relevant even today is however astonishing.

The idea of freedom of expression just extrapolates when the same gets applied to social media. Let's shift the point of view associated with social media and see it in a different light. It is a business platform, if not a product, which was curated with the aim to grow; namely by monetization of our 'likes' 'comments' 'shares' 'retweets'. While we keep viewing social media as a realm of free speech and expression, it is actually an arena which earns by monetizing us.

Before you make any speculations, let us make it clear, that we are in no way trying to say that it is a 'bad thing'. Social media started as an entrepreneurial venture and has now grown to be one of the biggest industries (which by the way is great). It has created new industries, opened up job opportunities and marketing arenas – another way to add to the economy and growth for the country. But let's just admit it for what it actually is and not epitomize it for something that it is not.

Now that this context has been set, let us decipher the idea of the so called 'freedom of expression'n social media. As discussed in the previous chapter 'Freedom', online freedom comes with a higher stake, given people get free tickets for cyber crime under the garb of anonymity. Instead of being a forum for open discussion and dialogue, free speech takes the form of, Threatening, homophobic, racist, sexist abuse which can actually stifle debate and lead to censorship – with some individuals not willing to say things that might provoke abuse. Columnist Owen Jones says that: "There's scrutiny of ideas, and then there's something else and trolling seems to be viewed as an acceptable price to pay for having a voice, for the illusion of freedom." The effect of free speech online is, perhaps, to "coarsen, even poison, political debate."

When we created a platform for people to share ideas, opinions, experiences and give voice to anything and everything, it comes with the baggage of their religious, political, social and every other controversial point of view. Even though this can be justified as an individual's personal point of view, the same when said by influencers, politicians, celebrities and anyone and everyone with mass following, creates problems.

For years, we have been talking about the opportunity and the threat of social media. It's ability to make and break ideologies. It's effectiveness to conquer something as big as elections, by creating propaganda or as small as to ***make you buy products***. While we all have reveled at the idea of an Arab springs and the use of social media to cause revolutions, we are all struggling now with the idea of social media causing genocide. The fact that social media is and has been used for ideology development to irk mass consciousness, just cannot be denied. It has been used as a space which demarcates 'us' and 'them'.

Today, services like Facebook Groups can also be a place where, for example, ethnic groups gather to form communities. Or Facebook Groups can become easy places for people to engage in identity tourism or as captive audiences for advertisers. Social media might be spaces for social protest where divergent political voices living in oppressive regimes might find a forum. Or social media may simply become spaces where divergent brand loyalties are contested and played out under the watchful eyes of corporations all too eager to exploit our desire to share our lives with our friends and families.

Myanmar, for instance, has an entire generation which is understanding internet and its potential. The same was used extensively to circulate anti- Rohingya messages leading up to the decade's worst refugee crisis. Human Rights activist

Zarni says, "Myanmar has a long ideological tradition by which genocides are acceptable." The fact that they were quoting Hitler left and right in the 1930's, proves this. With social media at their backs now, the propagation of hate has just become easier. The 2021 coup and the effects of protests and counter-protests within a community eager for censorship is astonishing.

Frankly, what did we expect? The value of nuclear electricity CANNOT be had without the threat of a nuclear bomb. It's the same with any new development, it's the same with AI, and it's certainly the same with social media.

One's man's revolutionary is another man's terrorist!

No one can disembark the potential of an invention as it can be easily swayed to become a miracle or a curse. This ability to feed the right kind of messaging to the right kind of people when they are in the right state of mind is the essence of marketing. Well, think of it. Marketing is about altering consumer behavior in favor of your desired action through positive confirmation. This is where the idea of data use and extraction achieves its relevance, right? Consumer behavior – the crux of it all. People and organizations have gone leaps and bounds to extract, understand and conquer it.

And social media has become the easiest possible medium for the same. It stands as an innovation which has the capacity to make and break. It works wonders for us at times and creates horrors for us at other times. What is the solution?

Control measures vs censorship

Social media and offline media are two totally different realms and both need to be dealt with in their own way. We don't want to live in an Orwellian reality where our every click, every transaction is recorded to curb 'anti-national' or anti-dominant-group activity. Though we are not saying that our data is safe and is not extracted for various marketing and political purposes (with or without our consent). The recent 'Facebook leak' incident (and we use this term loosely) has made it apparent. We are not saying that freedom should be curbed with content curtailed and blocked to suit the government's opinions and point of views (China being an example). Today the decision is in the hands of the giant tech platforms, where is the balance in that? The question is not whether the government should get to decide what the people see, the question is how can Twitter get to decide? (Indian IT Laws Debate 2021) And an even more important question is who gets to decide?

A way needs to be curated where cyber bullying and evidences of the same can be tracked and used for public interest. Both the social media platform creators and the watchdogs of the country need to contribute for an effective functioning. The platform developers/owners need to create parameters and guidelines to sort what should be promoted and what should be curtailed, what trends and what catches the eye. A common ground needs to be agreed upon by the two parties to safeguard both the business aspect and the social aspect of it all.

A good start is to enable people who are influencers and have verified profiles to prefix their social posts with fact, rumour, POV, analysis and cite sources. Wherever the source is not set right, it shouldn't be allowed. This becomes extremely crucial during political agendas and elections. While social media has the agency, as we mentioned, to make and break ideologies, let's use it to spread what is accurate and true to the core. Let's use it to the benefit of the country and humanity overall.

Who gets to decide is still debatable? May be we should empower the audience and lose all other controls.

Chapter 16

Create a Booming Tourism Industry

India, with several millennia of history, boasts of a diverse and rich built heritage. Each region of our subcontinent boasts of monumental buildings and remarkable archaeology. Yet, less than 15,000 monuments and heritage structures are legally protected in India—a fraction of the 600,000 protected in the UK. (Kant, Amitabh)

Being the world's longest continuing civilization, our country has a culture, history and heritage, which dates back to ages. The intra as well as the inter cultural interaction with the foreign lands have led to the crystallization of global discourses etched in the form of architecture on the Indian land. Be it an emperor's love for his beloved wife, a king's display of new conquered land or a warrior fortress built as an armour against the invaders all have assimilated to create a personification of the millennia-old history that our country has seen. We are perhaps second only to a small belt within the middle east in terms of our cultural mix spanning across centuries.

There has always been a question on as to why the vast cultural heritage has not been used enough to create a massive impact on India's GDP in form of the tourism industry. The question has been resonating for the past few years and with effect we have seen a tremendous growth. The 2017 *Travel and Tourism Competitiveness Report* by the World Economic Forum sees our country escalating from the rank of 65th position to 40th position in just three years.

The year 2016 touched new landmarks with 9 million tourists visiting the country. According to the World Travel and Tourism Council, the estimated revenue that came directly from the industry is around $208 billion, which was 9.6% of India's total GDP in 2016. It created over 40 million jobs which make 9.3% of our total country's population.

While this is definitely a great achievement, it is nowhere close to the potential our country has when it comes to the tourism industry. We have 29 states each having its own cuisine, language, history, visual attraction- in short our states individually have the calibre of an island or small country. Keeping this in mind 9 million international tourists seems a small number. When the city of Barcelona alone can attract a total of 8 million foreign tourists, just imagine the potential our country has with 4,000 cities.

Perception and inhibitors

While only 9 million tourists visited the country from abroad in the financial year 2016, the year witnessed 1.6 billion domestic tourists. The wide disparity in the number relegates down to the perception and the image that our country has worldwide.

Whether this stem from the exoticisation in western popular culture or the genuine experiences of the travellers, a perception of the country as a dirty place is widespread. There is no western depiction of India devoid of the sadhus or slums or poor half naked children. Even though the piece(s) might be inspired from a particular locality or old factual knowledge or just fiction, unfortunately, this is what our image as a country goes out.

We, however, cannot totally deny that the country needs aggressive cleanliness drive. There are enough examples of monuments being disfigured and vandalized, there are betel stains on 100 year old heritage or just structures being distorted.

Ranked as 106th safest country, safety issue remains to be another major factor. Recently, there have been a number of incidences which have brought to light the fate of international tourists, especially females. While this does depend from place to place, given the length and breadth of the country, there are some areas which require measures to safeguard the interest of foreign tourists.

The country's reputation took a serious beating with the second wave of coronavirus that started in mid-March 2021. The healthcare structure completely collapsed, at least that's what the coverage says. Interestingly, the total number of deaths in India are way lesser in percentage terms compared to a lot of western counterparts, even while accounting for less reporting. And, that's what perception does.

Hitting the bull's eye

The current travel and tourism industry of India is predicted to grow at an annual rate of 6.7% (pre-covid figures) and is estimated to generate revenue equal to 10% of the country's GDP by 2027. However, the industry has a potential of an annual growth rate of 30% which will eventually mean that it has the capability of contributing to 25% of India's GDP. Imagine adding a million additional jobs which would crop up of 20 million international travellers visit the country.

Following are a few steps/ ways which can help achieve the desired goal:

Swachch Bharat: Cleaning India remains to be of utmost responsibility. While the government initiatives are running in the backdrop, there needs to be a crowdsourcing model inviting volunteers to help clean the country up. A model where everyone comes together to do their bit

Tourism Board: When we define the tourist opportunities that we have because of the length and breadth of the country, we also have to keep in mind the hurdles that comes to synchronize the 29 states, 4,000 cities and 60,000 villages. Here is where the Tourism Board needs to step up to, clearly defining the goals and responsibilities of both the government and the private sector. The current scenario of being entirely self governed by multiple agencies has no common objective. All of them need to unite under the umbrella of Indian Tourism. Lets, for example, start by organizing and spreading the incredible India campaign, not in tattered bits and pieces, but actually integrate the national tourism with the state tourism.

Impact Tourism: The concept of impact tourism has been in circulation for a while. It aims to open up the 60,000 village culture to the travellers to give them an experience of a lifetime which is much more than just taking pictures. It aims to touch the soul with making the travellers staying in villages, making them taste authentic cuisines, making an unparallel connection through folklore and storytelling. While it enables the travellers to get beneath the surface, it also creates employment opportunities for the locals of the village

Perception Management: We need to elevate the image of the country. This need to be undertaken by both the managing the image and coming up with effort to remove the factor which cause that image. We need to have better safety measures and protocols for the travellers both domestic and international. Creating 24 hour helplines to deal with issues, improving infrastructure to curb the issue of last-minute connectivity are some of the steps that we can begin with.

More people visit the artificial pristine of Singapore than the natural beauty of India. Guess why?

Chapter 17

COVID-19, Environment & The Implications of World War III

Wikipedia defines World War as "a war engaged in by all or most of the principal nations of the world".

It doesn't have to be a war amongst each other. No one said a world war has to be a war between 2 warring factions of humans. It doesn't really need to be between countries, races, ethnicities or different sets of people. It doesn't need to have a winner and a loser. But what has happened since January 2020 is World War 3 (WWIII). An event that has impacted the whole world, brought people together (albeit socially distant), changed humanity forever, and is an ongoing fight for survival.

By all practical outlooks, Covid-19 is WWIII. Whether it has occurred due to a lab accident or whether it has been unleashed upon us by a maniacal regime, we would never know! But that doesn't change the fact that this is WWIII. Like the other wars, the traces of it will remain with us forever. Like the other world wars, power centers will emerge out of this one too.

The increased amount of virality and increased potency of COVID-19 vis-à-vis others in the last 50 years means this evolution couldn't have happened by itself. From slinging bodies during bubonic plagues over the fort walls to polluting the water bodies, the art of biological weapons is as old as human civilization itself. It may have reared its head in a globally connected world now, but the one to blame may just be increased globalization versus the weapon itself. From the Japanese use of bio-weapons in China and Manchuria, and the

Nazi use in concentration camps during Second World War to the mistaken release of Anthrax in Russia in 1970's, it has reared its ugly head multiple times in the past. Now we are adding a new phase to this.

The implications were unimaginable till we actually saw Covid. The ground underneath us has already shifted. By the time we get out of it, we would have evolved beyond imagination. Evolution being defined here as a change progressed over time. Good, bad or ugly – only time will tell. The actions we have seen over the years 2020 – 2021 are simply unprecedented. The question is whether it is an aberration or the signs of a changing world. That's the question everyone is asking.

I have believed for a very long time that the next world war (WW III) will not be a nuclear war, nor will it be a war fought with arms. It had to be a war of biological weapon or data as a weapon. Only this had the ability to impact the entire world at the same time. Whether its a natural occurring or artificial by accident or caused by someone, the impact is on each and every human across the globe. The biological war is currently upon us. The data war may come at a later date.

Fight against nature: We can never win. We can co-exist or get eliminated

The last few decades have been marked by widespread expansion of humans. Expansion of our numbers, expansion of our aspirations, expansion of the part of the earth we occupy but most importantly, expansion of the way we have tried to enslave nature.

Nature – the surroundings around us, the balance around us, the balance that keeps everything going, the balance that enables a peaceful co-existence of anything and everything around, a marvelous self-healing system that ensures the balance is always maintained.

That's what we have been banking on, that's what we have been wishing for subconsciously. But looks like we have overdone it. While nature will restore the balance, while we will be part of that balance or not, and in what form, is questionable. We have swung the pendulum beyond the nature's ability to self-heal and let humans continue the devastation.

It's important to point out the basic nature of evolution here amongst all species:

- The population of every species is self-regulated by nature through variety of balancing measures.
- There is a natural selection of the more capable one's and elimination of the dependent one's inherent in the nature. This leads to the concept of death and mortality. This also leads to fertility and the ability to reproduce amongst population. There is a reason why humans are born as 1 or 2, while dogs in multiples and rats in much higher numbers.

The population amongst humans right now is such that a small percentage of capable humans are carrying the burden of a larger percentage of less capable or dependent ones. This imbalance puts tremendous stress on the resources and the ability of the system to ensure existence. Whether it is through a natural or man-made incident, this imbalance is going to change. We all need to embrace that. Such is the nature of evolution.

This dynamics of this change have global ramifications. India is of course a cog in the wheel. With 1.3 billion people, and a rapidly growing importance in the global environment, an important cog in the wheel.

Chapter 18

The Rise of the Nazi China

You can agree or choose to disagree, but the reality of the current world is that China is the real deal. You may want to, choose to, hope to change that. But today the world runs on China. Everything in our life is dependent on them, not just our manufacturing but the entire supply chain for EVERYTHING.

In the past one year, ever since COVID-19 came into being, the whole world has witnessed one thing; that is, we are extremely reliant on CHINA. Be it medical equipment, or anything ranging from your daily use item like your mobile phones & cars to anything as complex as a microchip for satellites, China builds it all. This reliance is making it the biggest superpower in the world.

One truth is that they brought Covid-19 into the world, but an even bigger and more inconvenient truth is that they have only grown stronger from the pandemic. It doesn't matter if China's reported 5000 people died or 50,000 or 500,000. The fact is that they are exerting far more influence into the world everyday.

Most countries want to change that, some for geopolitical reasons, some for economic reasons, some for land and some just for the difference in ideologies. Multiple countries like US and India have touted that they're banning trade with China or altering their tactics to reduce reliance on China, but the unwavering amount of capacity that they possess to manufacture almost anything that you would want and everything that you would need has ensured that everything so far has backfired.

Even after facing constant flak from international communities and various developed and developing countries across the world, China just doesn't seem to be bothered. They understand that other countries are bound to lose more if they plan to sever ties with China and not vice-versa.

China has told the world loud and clear that they are not scared and that they are willing to go against international belief structures and orders. They are self-reliant and do not need an ounce of support from any other nation. On the 100th Anniversary of the Communist Party of China, their leader Xi Jinping alluded, China's rise is a "historical inevitability" and it will no longer be "bullied, oppressed or subjugated" by foreign countries. Anyone who dares to try, will find their heads bashed bloody against a great wall of steel forged by over 1.4 billion Chinese people"

India still has a blanket ban on Chinese imports but that's majorly for normal people like you and me and not for corporations or the government itself. The most that our country has done in terms of banning Chinese intervention in our economy is the banning of a few apps, which is more of a PR stunt than anything. The reality is even now India's Olympic jerseys (some may call it a matter of national pride) get sponsored by Chinese brands like La-Ning. Yes they get replaced after huge public hue and cry but that does nothing to alter our China dependence.

I have strongly maintained all along that the only way India or any other country can fight with China is by being competitive. The concept of bans do not work in free markets. They just cause some inconvenience. Being competitive requires way more than announcing multiple initiatives like Make in India & Aatmanirbhar Bharat. Urging people to switch to Indian products without taking into account the economic aspects and viability of the same is an absolute useless exercise.

Any country in a globally connected world can only succeed in being competitive by actually competing in a global environment. That will require a very focused concerted approach which the current democratic structure and the constant bickering and political fights in the US or India just can't provide. It's not about Modi or Trump or Biden or any other alternate, the fact is they just keep pulling each other down for small political mileages. Talk has become more important than the walk and thus the current state of affairs.

At the very beginning of the COVID-19 pandemic, I had talked about how it isn't important as to which country went into COVID lockdowns or when disaster struck them. The only thing that will govern the new order of the world is who comes out when. The earlier you are out, the earlier you will grow in the new order. This is where China gained further significance.

On 22nd March 2020, when India went into a complete nationwide lockdown along with many other countries that had locked down as well, China had already flattened its curve of COVID cases. US at that time was just starting to comprehend the real damage which came to fruition over the next few months with way over half a million people dying.

There is a significant amount of research around Coronaviruses that has happened in various parts of the world, significantly in Wuhan and North Carolina. It was not just specific to China, other countries(a.k.a. The United States) had a stake as well and were funding the research. Whether the virus was released on purpose or by mistake, it is clear that it is not a natural outbreak.

The Chinese aggression outlined in the South China Sea, the oppression in Xin Jiang, the increased connectivity with Tibet, increased border skirmishes with India, huge levels of loan debt to be an imperialistic power in weak underdeveloped countries (not all of them our neighbours), the increased buying out of ports, the necessitated need to own Taiwan(perhaps the only place that competes in semi-conductors) and the curbing of everything that happens in HongKong are clear demonstrations of what China is aiming for. The world so far has treated them with kid gloves. Seems like we have forgotten what happens when you let the unruly go rule.

The rise of Nazi China looks like our future.

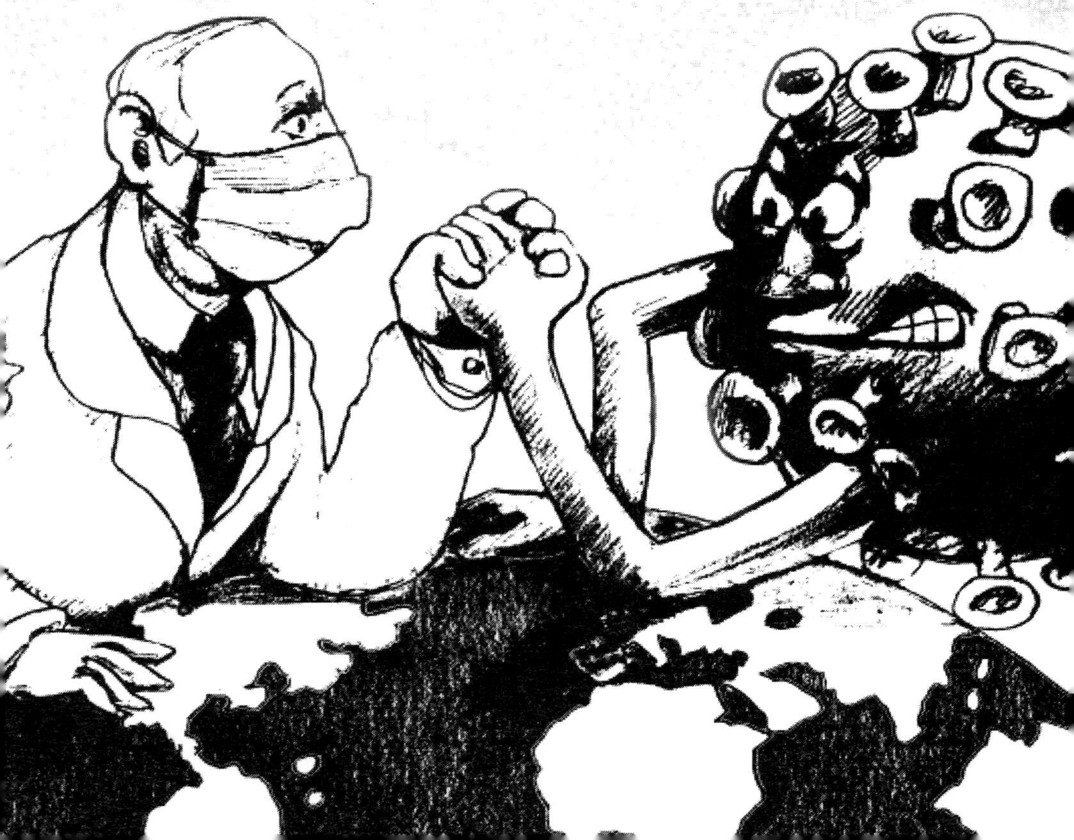

Chapter 19

Coronavirus Autocracies

"Those who would give up essential Liberty, to purchase a little temporary Safety, deserve neither Liberty nor Safety"

- Benjamin Franklin

When COVID-19 had just begun and the Peoples Republic of China went into a nationwide lockdown, the western world made much hue and cry about how it was undemocratic for them to lockdown a whole country against it's will and how it was a severe violation of human rights.

3 months later, all the big democracies had locked down their countries stripping their citizens of all forms of basic freedom, confining them to their homes on the premise of trying to save their lives. The government(s) become the owner of our lives, our mobility and our freedom?

In the past year, people across the world have gone through a series of lockdowns, government ordered quarantines and atrocities that some people argue were the need of the hour. During the first wave of the coronavirus in India, people were beaten, criminalised, kept in jails and were scarred for life only because they were thought to be COVID positive.

One thing that has happened during the course of the past one year is that people have gotten used to this way of life, of them being controlled by the government and of being stripped of their basic freedom for their good and for the greater good. It's a difficult proposition to argue whether such lockdowns were needed or not, I personally believe in a much more scientific natural selection and do not agree with those lockdowns, however, that is not really up for debate anymore.

The problem is that the governments across the globe have enjoyed the advantageous position that COVID-19 has put them in, wherein they can turn things into their favor using the epidemic act, lockdown anyone or any city they want, for as long as they want citing health concerns. Such absolute powers are very difficult to give up. This was the reason why the flawed system of democracy was adopted in the first place from the oppressive times of kings and autocrats and oligarchs of the roman and post roman empires.

If this trend continues, the democratic governments won't remain democratic anymore. More and more power over the people will be established by these democracies turned autocracies and it will lead to a misbalance in the society. If the lockdown is justified for Covid, if the taking away of personal freedom is acceptable because of a virus, how many other reasons can occur which may justify similar controls? How will we prevent democrats to become aristocrats and tyrants? How will we prevent such controls from being used against dissent? If gag order against a virus or a vaccine is in public interest, will a gag order against a mass murder not be issued in public interest? You are being told that your freedom is being taken away for the greater good. Does that sound alright to you?

This autocratic behavior is going to take away centuries of progression this human race has achieved and is going to result in revolutions, civil wars and freedom movements. The most worrying thing of all is that this blatant misuse of power is not happening in a war torn country or in just some obscure corner of the world. This is happening in the society as a whole, in the most developed countries and the world's biggest democracies and that is what makes it scary beyond belief.

Dictatorship has always been a revolutionary's refusal to give up power.

What if...
can't do it
wait
May be I can

Chapter 20

Mental Health

Mental health related issues have been around for as long as humanity has been around. For one thing that humans just can't do is shut up their mind. This is what distinguishes the alive from the dead.

As humanity moves towards prosperity, mental health issues start to surface more. This is because people have more time to think. It is because people become accustomed to a certain lifestyle (a way of living) and start doing everything to protect it.

We as humans spend our lifetime looking for stability and there is nothing that we hate more in our life than stability. It is status-quo that we have an issue with. We want change which comes in all shapes and sizes and with all flavors. For me personally, any move is progress, for most people there is a judgement around regressed or progressed.

So, what does mental health really mean. What does stress, anxiety, depression and the varied versions of issues we see, really come down to? In my view, the issues are of 2 kinds. Either they are chemical or they are social. We can't really distinguish one from the other always, it's a complex structure.

Most species live on 3 basic requirements from their species. Do they get the best of food, the best of community power and the best of mating? From other species, they have a simple requirement based on where in the food chain they fit. But we humans are not like that. We live in an extremely complex social structure and will do our best to defy any kind of order that our species may have lived with or evolved with over centuries. We are now translating ourselves into a species built on equality, a fact very hard for most to comprehend and perhaps impossible to implement. But we will continue our move towards that, like we all read in mathematics, N tending to Infinity (infinity being total equality). In a global interconnected environment, these complexities will continue to evolve, grow and make the solution harder.

This is what causes the underlying increase in the mental health issues that we see everywhere. I think of mental health issues like Coronavirus.

While not a virus, it's a disease that spreads faster than even the B1.617.2 version(and any subsequent, more transmissible mutations because it is not going away anytime soon) of Covid. There are people who are asymptomatic (only good to transfer the disease to others), then there are those with mild infection (they can do with some TLC and support), those with more severe infection (they need counseling and therapy) and then the critically ill ones (they need medication). All the while people suffering from mental health issues will continue to infect those around them.

There will never be a vaccine for it, so our best hope is to help generate some antibodies or some medicines that will reduce the spreading of the disease.

The most important correlation between Covid-19 and mental health issues is that unless there is a significant number of infected and identified people, and unless there is a full social acceptance, and unless there is concerted effort to improve the ones suffering from it, the ones who have it will not come out. They won't identify the problem for themselves and will simply keep suffering from it and infecting others.

This is where we as a society need to focus the most on. The viruses will come and go, other diseases will have a lifespan but the issues related to mental health need immediate and urgent intervention.

It is far truer now in a Covid wretched world and will be true in the post Covid world as well. A world where our entire social order has been disturbed. It's not a question of whether you contract Covid or not, your PTSD will be there just because your lifestyle was completely disturbed and more importantly because you lived in a non-social environment. It is now that the focus on mental health needs to be more.

For me, this is one area that I am willing to invest my life for. It will have layers to it. Social structure around is always going to be key and that is the missing piece always. In the absence of it, support has to start with ability for people to anonymously share whatever they are going through in life, further going into unrelated listening (talking to people who are not related to you but are going through or have just gone through a phase in life similar to you). Next level of it could be counseling and advice, going further into therapy and ending into medical help. One key is not just to provide treatment, rather it is to create people who can help others. This environment of better social structure where people around work with each other is the key to such transformation.

This exercise will be incomplete unless we mention the need to dumb down humanity a bit. Specially the travesties of 2020 & 2021 have shown how it's only the smaller things that matter and everything else is superficial. How we can live (and live well) without so much of what we call as must have.

In my view, we are at the cusp of a breakthrough. Humanity (forced or evolutionary) will go through this transformation of getting dumbed down over the next few years. Till then, working on mental health is they key to survival and perhaps the key to ensuring everything else is in place.

Chapter 21

Retirement

I have always believed that a human life is to be forever progressive. Growing from one aspect to the other. This growth is unique to people. No two humans will traverse the same path. With this mindset, I have always maintained that I will never retire.

While I still maintain that, the concept of retirement and old age need to be explored more fully in its traditional definition. In the past 100 years, healthcare has come a long way, and as a result, life expectancy has increased tremendously. People easily have a life span of 65+ years these days in most parts of the world as compared to 25-30 years back in the 1920s. While this is great news and it clearly demonstrates that we are developing with time, it also poses a problem that most often than not goes unnoticed. This change in social structure and society is causing some unforeseen complexities.

We have always lived in a world where there is a fear of death. In my view, there is an urgent need to take away that fear and replace it with something better. Specially with the increasing age of people. The old age FOMO is worse than any teenager's obsession with being the center of attention and participating in everything.

As a system, there should be a specified number, an age after which a person cannot work for monetary benefits, for financial gain. This shouldn't apply to just corporates, it should hold true for CEOs, politicians and any other similar leadership positions. Now, I am not of the opinion that these people should be left high and dry and that they shouldn't be doing anything. Instead, I am proposing that they take on the role of mentors, become a guiding power to their younger counterparts and advise for the remaining part of their lives or till the time they choose to participate.

There is a need to formulate mentorship programs that will serve the purpose of making retired people take the next step towards a life that is void of responsibility. Old people do need support to enjoy the latter part of their lives and to have financial independence. All of that needs to be taken care of if there's not going to be any money involved as I have pointed out before. To begin with, fix the maximum age upto which a person can have the role of the CEO or the role of a parliamentarian and so on.

The function of life is forever progressing. The Hindu philosophy talks about the progression of life and how taking Sanyaas is not about going away, it is more about giving up and growing up. Sanyaas is essentially giving up working for financial gains and starting to work for the greater good. It doesn't necessarily mean that you have to leave your family and go to a far away place, it just means that you have to let go of your power and focus your energy on providing mentorship and support to others that need it or are now in charge. Working to create better versions of yourself for the skills that you perfected over the years.

When that age is gone, there should not be a fear of going away. In my personal view, Euthanasia should be a standard practice and should be promoted extensively. If you have no usefulness of your life, for you and for others, why won't you choose to go away. May be there is something better waiting for you on the other side. For believers of heaven or for believers of reincarnation or for believers of science of constant evolution, it must be a fascinating and curious thought. At least, I look at it that way. The day I become irrelevant and useless in this world, I would choose to go away from this world, to whatever is next.

Conclusion

I first wrote this chapter on 31st December 2018. The last day of the year. And I saw a new world order emerging. Back then, perhaps the 3 most convoluted and unstable countries in the developed/developing world were the US (Trump), UK (Brexit) and France (anti-Macron). Now that Trump is behind us or at least not in front of us, Brexit is done, France is headed for elections and most importantly, we have all seen COVID-19. The world is never going to be the same again.

At the time of writing, India has just gotten out of the 2nd wave of COVID. Almost every family has seen setbacks, grief has been experienced by all those who we have always wanted to protect. Kids haven't gone to school for more than a year and the debate between work from home and going to office is ripe.

At its core, the world will go through a bigger change in the next 20 years than it has in almost the entire humanity of 5000 years. Some key aspects of this change I foresee are as follows:

- **Ownership:** The 2 largest investments people have in their lives are real estate and cars. While these will continue to be tools rich people will keep to store their assets, they will lose significance otherwise. Pay per usage model will become prevalent enabled by technology and hence no need for ownership.
- **State Responsibilitie**s: The state will consume / subsume responsibility for numerous life's requirements and hence the overall income requirement will be low. This will be most significant in aspects like local transport, electricity, network connectivity, basic food items, basic housing, etc.

- **Income:** With the state being responsible for much, income levels will go down significantly. People will be able to live with little to no income and won't need to pay for much of the stuff.
- **Mobilization:** The overall mobilization of people will go down. Technology will enable a world where globalization won't require mobilization. Hence, the social structures will become more rigid. People will be able to interact, visit and engage using technology. With technology, both leisure as well as business travel will decrease. Air-travel and cross country travel will become cost prohibitive for masses. There will be much higher levels of scrutiny for travelers. These were our thoughts in a pre-covid world but Coronavirus and the corresponding lockdowns and changes over the last 2 years have rampantly increased the rate of this change. We thought this change will be driven by terrorism, will be driven by the fighting humans. Little did we realise, we won't need any fighting humans for this to happen. Because of Corona, Insurance and medical check-ups will become mandatory and account for some of the cost increase in travel.
- **Population:** With technology pervasiveness, the overall requirement of the number of people hence the population will go down. Contribution as human or dependent: The ones contributing will move further. The dependent ones will get eliminated. Simple rule of evolution and survival. Explains the impact of COVID-19 on older population. Some may even call this nature's fight back.
- **Meaning of life:** Forever progressing, forever moving. If you aren't, you shouldn't be there. This need to become the theme for everyone and everything. Need to talk about equilibrium. The equilibrium is the present. It is not good or bad. It is what is. And we keep looking for what better. But it's the equilibrium. You maybe rich or poor, healthy or sick, alone or surrounded, this or that, whatever it is becomes the equilibrium of your life. Lockdown is an amazing proof of people's ability to adapt to the new equilibrium.
- **New power centers in the world will emerge:** China is in line to become the new power center of the world. Other new centers will be in Africa

and Asia as well but that's further away. At the top level, the countries which will be able to shrink themselves into more sustainable units will progress more, unless we go to a robotic world. Please note there is a stronger chance of humans becoming robots (or robot like) versus robots becoming humans.

- **Changing face of communities:** Closed, self-sufficient, independent communities will be formed. If you think about the lockdown we lived in, what is the total cost of living and what do we need. This is a huge subject and need much deliberation. People need food, shelter and clothes. Add a stable ubiquitous internet connection and we are done. A lot of other aspects of life sit on the fringes as frivolities. There will be a move towards basics. Farming and food processing industry will become the most important sectors

Its going to be an exciting time going forward. Of course, the thought of humanity destroying humanity will always exist. Till then, let's roll on!

About the Authors

KAPIL GUPTA

A marketeer to the core, Kapil Gupta is an entrepreneur, both in thought and in style who believes that the power of a message & its delivery is what causes true revolutions. Kapil Gupta is a parallel entrepreneur who believes in providing true meaning to the various organizations he runs and builds them in sync with one another. He jokingly calls himself the jack of all trades and a master of some. He is the Founder and the CEO of *OMLogic* (India's leading digital marketing agencies), *PragatiE* (a virtual exhibition platform), *Frontlist* (portal for the publishing industry), *Solh* (a mental wellness platform & his current passion project), *Advit Toys* (a board games company).

Kapil is a true believer in new-age equality, which for him is deep-rooted in providing equal opportunity to all. He believes that the current world of equality is still a 20th century way of working, which is rotten with personal benefits in the forms of subsidies & reservations (women, LGBTQ, religion, race, caste, region based). For true equality, everybody MUST be treated equally. Period. This has put him quite at odds with what he calls as the current brand of pseudo-feminists, pseudo-liberals and pseudo-social-activists. The liberals find him too conservative and the conservatives find him too liberal, yet he doesn't associate himself as a centrist at all. For him, the classification in the current world has gone awry and a new brand of ideologies has to appear. Kapil runs a weekly video programme called '*Truth Shots with Kapil*', where he delves deeper into the various topical or everyday social issues.

Uninspiringly yet comfortably dressed in shorts, t-shirts and floaters, Kapil hates to dress-up for almost any occasion. A person who enjoys a fine scotch on the rocks, you are always welcome to have an argument, but make sure you have some time in your hand cause he might get really passionate about his cause. It's not even a joke!

BHUSHAN BHATI

A born critic, Bhushan has been analyzing things since he was 10. A 22-year-old journalism graduate, you might wonder what he knows about the world & you will be right, not much, but enough to make a difference. His ability to simplify things gives him an edge when it comes to communicating with the masses. A behind the doors activist, the reason why he has authored this book is because he believes in unlearning. Another reason why he chose to work with Kapil is because they seldom agree on anything, which is why they have been able to fine tune this book.

A debater of sorts, Bhushan is known to never back down from an argument, no matter how heated it may get, provided that he knows what he is speaking about, because do keep in mind that he is still learning. His experiences in life have been starkly different than anybody else, an entrepreneur at 13, he built a business from scratch when most kids were just playing video games, and surprisingly in the field of video games. A communicator and a people's person, he is currently working as an EA to Kapil and hopes to delve into the world of public policy once he has grown enough, both in terms of knowledge and understanding.